Forex Trading

The best simple strategies for beginners. The basics system trading for earning money online. Learn the way to trading currency and the right money management

Author Name:

Andrew Steve Hammer

Table of Contents

Introduction

Forex trading is also known as the foreign exchange market. This foreign exchange market is vast, and it comprises investors from different institutions, governments, banks, corporates, and all currency speculators. Therefore forex trading is the exchanging of different currencies at a profit. Any currency in the world is exchanged to another for any foreign trade to be carried out successfully.

For example, tourists from Jamaica going to the United States of America for a holiday will have to exchange their Jamaican dollars into American dollars. This exchange will enable them to buy anything they want and have a comfortable stay with the American dollars to spend. Also, if any trader from France wants to buy cocoa from Ghana, he will change his money from the French currency, euros to Ghanaian currency, Ghanaian Cedes. This changing will be helpful for the trade to be complete.

Chapter 1: Forex Trading Basics

The exchange of the currency in the international markets makes sure that the transaction is done at the equivalent values of the market price. If a dollar is selling or buying at 100 cedes in Ghana, this means, any Ghanaian trader who wants to convert his money, will use the current value of 100 for his money. The currencies conversion rates keep changing from time to time. They can change in a day or two or even take months. This change is due to the economic balance of the country and many other factors that determine currency stability.

This international markets exchange is very explicit on centrality. It does not compress the trade to any central point. There is no specific market place where the foreign exchange takes place. The foreign exchange trade is generally made electronically, and it trades the securities of the companies that are not formally listed, also known as Over the Counter (OTC). All the transactions in this trade happen through computer networks amongst traders in the whole world and not on a specified exchange that is at a central point.

The foreign exchange markets are always open and work from Monday to Friday and half day on a Sunday. In these days, all the exchange of currencies is done in the major centers cross all time zone. There are nine major final exchange centers that the transaction happens in the 24 hours daily of the five and half days of the week. These centers are Zurich, Frankfurt, Tokyo, Hong Kong, Singapore, New York, Paris, and Sydney. These financial centers allow the forex trade to go on without stopping. If the trade-in Hong Kong comes to an end, the business in the U.S.A is starting. So it is a rotational process that allows traders to trade around the clock.

People should, therefore, understand that forex trading is very different from the stock markets. Forex trade is a new market compared to the stock markets that started centuries ago. It also involves the conversion of currencies only, without having to buy any securities and sell them from any company. Traders going into this business should have a clear understanding of what forex trading means, not just literally but practically before they invest their money.

There are different benefits of trading in forex, every trader has his objectives of the trade, and therefore various benefits fits different trader's goals.

Reasons as To Why One Should Trade Forex

Ability to go short

Trading forex enables you to go short in other markets. You can always go short using benchmark products like cumulative distribution function. Short selling is amongst the best and essential qualities of forex trading. In short sale, you can sell the second currency in the direct and indirect pairs. This action is commonly known as the quote or counters currency. After selling your quote money, you can purchase another currency called the transaction currency or the base currency. A forex pair price is determined by how much a unit of the transaction currency is worth in the counter currency.

Flexible Trading Hours

Forex trade takes five and a half days in trading. It starts from Sunday 9.00 pm to Friday 10.00pm, Greenwich Mean Time. When a major center in one comes to an end, there is always another center open. Since forex trade is not central pointed, but over the counter, it gives traders flexibility in trading. A trader does not have to wait for a closed session to start so that he can trade. He can always trade with the open, active sessions during the trading hours.

Traders should note that, despite the flexibility in trading hours of the foreign exchange, the opening hours of the markets sometimes vary especially in March, April, October, and November. The reason for the variation in opening hours is because the different countries shift differently on daylight saving. It is crucial for retail traders also to understand that during the weekend, they are not allowed to trade. All markets in the forex market close on Friday at 10.00 pm, United Kingdom Time, and opens on Sunday evening at 9.00pm, United Kingdom Time.

The lack of trading on the weekend of the forex market can cause a difference in the prices. The difference between Friday when the prices close and Sunday when the prices open is called a gap. This gap can be an increase in prices in the forex market or a decrease in the prices. This means traders should be very keen on the trading hours of the weekend and change their positions according to the trend.   Not being aware of this puts a trader's position at the gapping risk.

High Liquidity

Foreign exchange has so many investors globally, and it entails long hour's activeness. This character makes it the most liquid market. Traders trading all the time makes the market very active. Vast amounts of money are traded daily. An estimate of 5 trillion dollars is converted daily by companies, corporates, and individuals to get profits from the trade.

Forex Volatility

Forex trading involves the transaction of enormous money. Billions of dollars are exchanged daily while trading, and this makes the movement of prices volatile. Traders can make huge profits when some of the currencies become volatile by predicting price trends. He can also switch and choose any currency that he feels comfortable trading with and the one he believes will give him good profits.

Nonetheless, traders must be careful and are equally risky. In the prediction of reaping huge profits, and a trader is likely to get massive losses if the direction of the prices is not well predicted. Traders should manage the risk while investing by using different risk management tools.

Leverage is an Advantage towards Money Growth

Different foreign exchange companies give leverages while trading the pairs. When companies give leverage, they make traders money grow. The leverage helps the trader to pay a small amount in of what he is required to pay in the currency market when opening a position. This amount is paid up front. When a trader trades on this leverage margins, he has better chances o getting huge returns on the small investments he put in. The profits or the losses he gets after the closing of this investment shows the full value of his position.

In as much as the trader can get huge returns on the small investments, he is also likely to incur losses. The margin he is trading in catalyzes the losses and these losses can exceed the trader's upfront amount that he deposited. This mostly happens with traders trading with CFDs. Therefore, traders should be keen when trading with the Cumulative Distribution Functions.

They should put into consideration the total value of the position leveraged before trading.

No or Low Commissions

Everyone wants to save money, no matter how little it is. Forex trading gives you a chance to save some money that you could have used to by the commissions to brokers of other businesses. Forex trading has meager commissions charged by the forex traders compared to other trade brokers. When the dealers do not involve the brokers, there are commission charges, and there is also no clearance fees making the trade the better option to trade.

Trade More Currency Pairs

Different variety of currency pairs is traded in forex trading. The trading of these pairs speculates on the world's events and how strong the major and the minor economies are around the world. Different companies like IG gives the trader the freedom to choose from over 90 currency pairs to trade with. The currency pairs offered by the company include;

- Emerging currency pairs, e. g USD/CNH, EUR/RUB, and AUD/CNH. This currency pairs are upcoming. These currencies are trying to gain some popularity in the forex markets.

- Exotic Currency Pairs. This pair includes but not limited to EUR/CZK, TRY/JPY, and USD/MXN. These currency pairs comprise a major currency like the USD working together with an emerging currency pair like the MXN. These exotics are very beneficial for they give huge returns, especially when the prices go down, but they are high risk to trade with.

- Minor Currency Pairs, e. g, USD/ZAR, SGB/JPY, CAD/CHF, EUR/GBP, NZD/JPY. These are the currency pairs that do not have the US Dollar (USD) on either side of the exchange, but they contain a major currency. For example, the NZD conversion against the JPY. The Japanese Yen is a major currency.

- Major Currency Pairs, e. g EUR/USD, GBP/USD, USD/CHF (Swiss Francs), USD/CAD, AUD/USD. The major currency pairs the most traded. The pairs contain the American Dollar as the base or the quote currency.

All the currency pairs are available, and a trader can use a single account to login in and start trading. A trader can decide to use any currency to trade as per his trading style.

Forex Hedging

Positions can encounter unwanted moves from foreign exchange rates. This moves put the positions at risk, and a forex hedge can help in reducing this risk. It opens up more potential positions. A forex hedge helps protect a trader who deals with long a foreign currency pair from a downward risk. It can be used by different traders, like the market participants, investors, traders, and businesses. On the other hand, a forex hedge helps traders trading with short currency pairs against the upside risk.

Control over the trade

Since there are a variety of currency pairs to trade with, the trader controls what he wants to trade in without any force. The trader asses the risks and the potential returns himself and makes a decision solely of whether to enter the trade or not. The power of trading lies entirely in the trader's hands.

Allows Practice

Unlike most trades, forex trade has a demo account. This demo account helps a trader practice on how to analyze the trend and how to invest their money. Forex trading demo account equips the trader with enough knowledge and skills of the forex market before the real deal. It helps the trader make a clear decision of whether to join the trade or not. It is like being given an exam paper with a leakage.

Information Transparency

You must have come across trades that hide some information and take it as an advantage to get more returns. Forex trading is the total opposite of these other trades. In forex trading, despite being a broad market has the fairest information transparency. With the markets size, the fire trade makes sure that the information reaches the traders, maybe not on the exact time but the required time because of the difference in the time zones.

Low Transaction Costs

Forex trading deals with direct dealers. This means there is no brokerage fee, unlike the other trades. The trade gives a lot of options with the meager investment cost making it more advantageous. The direct dealers involving themselves in the business make the prices cheaper than other markets. Generally, forex trade is free from commissions, exchange fees, government fees, and the brokerage fee.

Low Entry Fee

When most people hear of the forex trade, they shun away from it thinking that it is a trade-off he mighty. They need to prove wrong this assumption. Forex trading requires little capital to start when compared to trading in stocks and options. The online brokers in the currency exchange trade offer an account with a minimum affordable amount like $25.

Globalization

Foreign exchange trade entails trading worldwide. This trade promotes globalization which helps in strengthening the social ties between different countries and different people. This globalization also helps the trader get more knowledge of various trades in different countries. Different ideas will; be exchanged during forex trading, which helps in business and self-growth of the trader.

Risk-Free Demos

Demo accounts that a trader uses for his practice are free and do not affect your money in any way. The money in the demo account can all be lost without any effect on your money. The demo account helps those who want to know what the trade entails practically before getting into it. The risk here is zero.

Trade Flexibility

After the trader mastering what the trade entails and how to invest, he can choose from the currency pair any currency pair to trade with. The business is so flexible that no restrictions are put on the choice of currency pairs to use in your trade. The trade also allows people from different places to share ideas without any restrictions making it more flexible and better amongst other trades.

Largest Financial Market

The fact that forex trading is the largest financial market gives it an added advantage of more investors. The stability of any market brings in more investors. When more investors bring in money, there are high chances of anyone to get high gains from their investments.

When is the Forex Market Open?

Time is a significant factor in everything we encounter in life. In forex trading, time is a very crucial ingredient to the success of your trade. The foreign exchange markets are always open, 24 hours a day.

Knowing the time of opening the trade is essential, but mastering the right time of trading is more important.

The best time a trader should put up a sail and start trading is when the markets are very active. It means there are significant volumes that he can trade in giving him an excellent opportunity to make good returns on his investment.

Forex Trading Hours

MAJOR CENTRES	OPEN	CLOSE	OPEN TIME ZONE	CLOSED TIME ZONE
New York	8.00 am	5.00 pm	EST/EDT	GMT+1
Tokyo	7.00 am	4.00 pm	EST/EDT	GMT+1
Sydney	5.00 am	2.00 am	EST/EDT	GMT+1
London	3.00 am	12.00 Noon	EST/EDT	GMT+1

Within these trading hours, some hours overlap. The overlapping hours fall between;

- New York and London: 8.00am to Noon EST/EDT

- Sydney and Tokyo: 7.00 pm to 2.00 am EST/EDT
- London and Tokyo: 3.00 am to 4.00 am EST/EDT

During the above overlapping time, traders can utilize these hours to get more gains in the trade. At this time the volumes of the business are high, and there is a lot of activity (trading) taking place.

Brokers with the forex trading Hours

Forex brokers are the mediators in the exchange trade. The brokers create different platforms for forex trading. When it comes to trading hours, the forex broker gives you his working time with the trading platform he offers. The broker's time is dependent on the time zone of his country where he works.

If you do not want to get mixed up with the trading time, do not follow the time provided by the broker on the platform but put your focus on the universal clock (EST/EDT). Alternatively, you can use the market Hours monitor to know when the trade is in session.

The actual opening time or closing time depends on the local time of the major centers — the hours of opening and the closing difference in March, April, October, and November. The reason behind the time variation here is because some countries move from or to DST-Day

Time Saving. The other major centers experience the Day Time Saving apart from Japan.

Summarily, forex trading is a risky trade, but one can as well get good huge returns. You will hate the business if you do not understand the rules of the game. Sometimes, the losses exceed the money you invest. This does not mean the trade is bad. It means you need to go back to the drawing board and look to the rules of the game once more .you need to understand this trade very well before investing in your money. You can start with the demo. It doesn't matter how much time you take to master the trade skills, and the most important thing is to understand what you want to get into before investing.

Chapter 2: What Do We Trade-In the Forex Market?

Forex Pairs

They are also known as the currency pairs. When one value's currency is quoted against the value of another currency, this quotation is known as the currency pairs. The currency pair is a unit of the foreign exchange trade. It is an instrument which traders buy and sell in the business.   There are different types of currency pairs represented by the base currency and the quote currency.

Base Currency

You probably have guessed what a base currency pair is by understanding the word base. The name base itself represents solidity. This definition is not different in the base currency pair. The base currency pair precedes any other currency when being transacted. The use of the currency pairs quotes currency unit prices in the market. The base currency – also called the transaction currency - is the first currency appearing in a currency pair quotation, followed by the second part of the reference, called the quote currency or the counter currency. In accounting calculations, most entities use base currency as their primary currency to represent the losses a d the profits in the companies.

In forex, the base currency shows how much of the quote currency you require to get one unit of the base currency. For example, if you were looking at the EUR/JPY currency pair, the base currency, in this case, will be the Euro and the Japanese Yen will be the quote currency.

In forex trading currencies are contemporary bought and sold at a profit against the other at all times. If a trader buys a currency pair, he will be purchasing the base currency and selling the quoted currency inherently. The buying price, also known as the bid price shows how much value of the quote currency you need to get one unit of the base currency. Inversely, when a trader sells the currency pair, will be selling the base currency and in return, he gets the quote currency.

When a trader sells a unit of the base currency, it will show the selling price of the currency pair being represented by the amount the trader got from the quote currency. The forex trade is very different from the stock trade. While a trader is using another currency here to buy the other, in the stocks, the traders use cash to purchase the shares.

ISO decides the forex trade abbreviations. The International Standardization Organization. The International Standardization Organization provides these codes in the standard ISO 4217. These codes represent all the currency pairs. The three letters from the codes represent the currencies. Sometimes, currencies separation is shown by a slash or a dash when showing the conversion between the two currencies. The base currency is the first then a slash or dash, followed by the quote currency. You may find other currency pairs without the dash or the slash character.

There are major and minor currencies codes. The major currency codes include USD for the United States dollar, the euro abbreviated as EUR, JPY a representation of the Japanese yen, the British pound-GBP, the Australian dollar-AUD, the Canadian dollar-CAD and lastly the Swiss franc abbreviated as the CHF.

The rules that come up with the currency pair's notations must be first accepted before they are used.

The rules are the priorities received by all the currencies being used in the forex trade.

Since the beginning, the European Central Bank ruled out that the euro abbreviated as the EUR must take the first place in the currency pairs. It is a base currency in any transaction of the foreign exchange trade that it features in. The EUR must be listed first then followed by the other currency it is being transacted with. For example, if the United States dollar is being negotiated with the euro exchange, then the rate of exchange is shown as EUR/USD. If the Japanese Yen is being transacted with the euro, then the denotation will be EUR-JPY or EUR/JPY.

Quote Currency

This currency is also known as the counter currency or the secondary currency. This currency comes second in the currency pair, whether indirect or direct. The quote currency is as essential as the base currency. The quote currency aids in the determination of the base currency value. When the quote currency is used in an indirect quote, it represents the foreign currency, but when a quote currency is used in a direct quote, it represents the domestic currency.

The rate of exchange of any currency pair shows how much value of the quote currency is needed to be sold so that one unit of the base currency is bought. When the rate of the currency pair increases during trading, the value of the quote currency falls in both the foreign currency and the domestic currency.

For example, the cross rate between the Euro denoted as EUR, and the Japanese Yen indicated as JPY is shown as USD/JPY. It means the Japanese Yen is the quote currency that is determining the value of the euro, which is the base currency. The Japanese Yen is a reference currency to the Euro. When this trade between the euro and the Japanese yen denoted as USD/JPY takes place, the JPY is considered the foreign currency by the United States while the USD is the domestic currency.

Alternatively, if the euro trades with the United States dollar, then the cross rate between the two is an indirect quote denoted as the EUR/USD. The euro being ruled out as the preceding currency pair by the Europe Central Bank, in this case, it is the base currency while the United States dollar is the quote currency. The United States dollar here helps in the determination of the value of the Euro, making it the domestic currency.

Types of Currency Pairs

There are different types of currency pairs in the forex market that traders use during trading. Note, the currency pair should not be confused with the base currency and the quote currency. The base and the quote currency are the units used in the exchange of each other. When a trader is buying and selling, the base currency and the quote currencies are involved. This same trader will be trading using a particular currency pair that he is comfortable to trade with. In simpler terms, the base currency and quote currency are compulsory in the forex trading while the currency pairs are optional. A trader can choose from amongst the many.

Major Currency Pairs

The major currency pairs are the most active currency pair. This currency pair is the most traded currency pairs in the forex trading. There are four most traded currency pairs in the foreign exchange market.

These five major currency pairs being the most traded currencies are part of the ten most traded currencies and most liquid currencies in the world. The group is commonly known as the g10 currency group. These major currency pairs carry out vast volumes of transactions across the forex market. Most traders prefer using the major currencies believing that they will get better returns when they invest their money in the trade.

Most people consider the major currency pairs because they lead the global forex market, have high volumes, and are the most heavily traded currency pairs. It is said that the major currency pairs consist of only four major pairs. Research says some people in an extensive part of the world trading in the forex believe that the transaction between the United States Dollar and the Canadian Dollar denoted as USD/CAD, Australian Dollar and United States Dollar, AUD/USD, and New Zealand dollar transaction and United States Dollar pairs should be added to the list of the major currency pairs.

These currency pairs are also heavily traded across the globe. Sometimes their trading volumes often exceed that of the two currency pairs in the significant market, United States transaction with Swiss Franc, USD/CHF and the British pound transacting with the United States dollar, GBP/USD. These there, despite people wanting them to be regarded among the major currency pairs, they belong to another group called the commodity pairs.

The major currency pairs are;

- The United States Dollar- USD.

- The Euro-EUR

- The Japanese Yen- JPY

- The British Pound-GBP

- The Swiss Franc-CHF

The most traded currency pair around the globe is the euro and the United States Dollar, EUR/USD. This currency pair represents more than 20% of transactions in the forex market. The second widely and heavily traded currency pair is between the United States Dollar and the Japanese Yen, USD/JPY. This currency pair is followed by the British pound transacting with United States Dollar, GBP/USD, and lastly the United States Dollar Transaction with the Swiss Franc, USD/CHF.

Every currency in the primary currency has the United Stated Dollar on either of the side. Either AS a base currency or a quote currency. The reason for this is because the United States Dollar is the leading reserve currency in the market.

Minor Currency Pairs

These are the currency pairs that do not have the United States Dollar on either side. They are also known as the cross-currency pairs. These currency pairs are comprised of less popular instruments, unlike in the major currency pairs. The currencies included in this minor currency pairs are of local value with their liquidity coming from the United States Dollar and the Euro. The minor currency pairs include;

- The Euro is transacting against the British pound-EUR/GBP.

- The Euro is transacting Versus the Australian Dollar- EUR/AUD.

- The British Pound is transacting against the Japanese Yen- GBP/JPY.

- The Swiss Franc is transacting against the Japanese Yen- CHF/JPY.

- The New Zealand Dollar is transacting against the Japanese Yen-NZD/JPY.

- The British Pound Transacting versus the Canadian Dollar- GBP/CAD.

The cross rates of the cross over currency pairs are easy to calculate using the main pairs. For example, if you want to calculate the standard in the transaction between the Euro and the British Pound, you delete the United States Dollar in the trade between the Euro and the United States Dollar EUR/USD and also remove the United States Dollar in the transaction between the British Pound and United States Dollar, GBP/USD currency pairs. The Euro- EUR, the Japanese Yen-JPY, and the British Pound-GBP are the most traded minor currency pairs around the globe.

Exotic Currency Pairs

Exotic currency pairs are not easily found. These currency pairs comprise if currencies of developing countries and the major currencies. For example, the currency of countries like Ghana, South Africa, Mexico, Singapore, and Brazil combined with the major currencies forms exotic currency pairs. When trading, the spread in the exotic currency pairs are high, and you are only likely to find the major currency pairs and the minor currency pairs. Below are the commonly traded Exotic Currency Pairs;

- The Euro trading against the Turkish Lira-EUR/TRY.

- The United States Dollar is transacting versus the Hong Kong Dollar-USD/HKD.

- The Japanese Yen trading verses the Norwegian Krone-JPY/NOK.

- The New Zealand Dollar is transacting against the Singapore Dollar-NZD/SGD.

- The British pound trading verse the South African Rand- GBP/ZAR.

- The Australian Dollar is transacting against the Mexican Peso.

Below is a table showing the exotic currencies transacting against each other.

Exotic Currency Pairs Table:

CURRENCY PAIRS	
EUR-TRY	Euro versus Turkish Lira
USD-HKD	United States Dollar Versus Hong Kong Dollar
JPY-NOK	Japanese Yen Versus Norwegian Dollar
NZD-SGD	New Zealand Dollar versus Singapore Dollar
GBP-ZAR	British Pound Versus South African Rand
AUD-MXN	Australian Dollar Versus Mexican Peso

A trader who wants to trade with exotic currency pairs should be keen enough. He should have sufficient knowledge and experience of the forex trade. If not, he should stick to trading with the minor currency pairs and the major currency pairs. The major and minor currency pairs will give a trader an easier time to trade with. They have lower spreads compared to the exotic currency spreads, which has very high spreads and are less liquid. However, traders who have enough experience in the forex trade and who understand the exotic currency pair trade can get very reasonable returns despite the pairs being riskier than the majors and the minors.

Forex Trading Platforms

There different places where forex trade takes place. This trade is done electronically. Different traders look at various trading soft wares to choose the best platform to trade with. The traders can always decide which platform they want to trade with. However, before selecting a platform to trade with the traders are required to understand and follow some trading steps to help them not to curse the trade immediately after investing their money. These steps are like a road map to the final destination. The following steps should be followed by any trader who wants to trade in the foreign exchange.

Choosing a Currency Pair

A trader should make up his mind which currency pair is more suitable for him. There are so many currency pairs that one can trade with, but it is very critical to choose a trading currency pair that you feel comfortable with. Picking a trading currency is sometimes hard, but there are different analysis tools, both technical and fundamental, that help a trader pinpoint a trading opportunity that can suit his style of trading.

Traders should put in mind the volatility of different currency pairs and the risk ratio before selecting any pair to trade with. Other currency pairs have huge potential returns but very risky. A trader should choose a currency pair with low risk, or manageable risk and reasonable returns than the one with huge profits with high risks. Most traders go for the major and minor currency pairs in this case.

Make a Decision on Your Trading Style

Traders mostly trade with the city index Spread Betting -CISB, the Contract for difference-CFD, or Forex trading. These threes styles have different amounts to be invested in. A trader should choose which method he wants to trade in and is comfortable with. For example, if a trader wants to trade pounds per point, then he will have to choose the City Index Spread Betting trading style.

Have a Clear Decision on Purchases and Sales

You should have a formed mind of whether you are entering the business to sell or to buy. You do not want to join the trade and be stagnant, not knowing which direction to take. You will buy your currencies if your prediction of the base currency is going to be stronger than the quote currency. You will have to sell the currencies you bought once your forecast shows that the quote currency is going to weaken in value against the base currency or it has started decreasing in value.

Add Orders

There are different orders in the forex trade. A trader can use the stop the losses or limit these losses while trading using the stop-loss orders and the limit loss orders. This orders will help a trader get the expected profits even when the loss risk or profit target is reached. Adding these orders to your trade is very important because you never when the business will incur a loss.

Monitor and Close Your Trade

The price movement in the market determines the profits or the losses of open trade. A trader should update his potential incomes in time. This activity can only be done through monitoring your business and closing it if the prices are dropping on time to avoid more losses.

Close Your Trade

By closing your trade, your net loss or profit will be seen in your account. It is the opposite of how you opened the business. If you traded with 5 CIBS, this means your trade was open, to close it, you sell your 5 CIBS.

Types of Trading Platforms

Meta Quotes Platforms

Meta Quotes Platforms are the most common type of platforms that brokers offer to clients to trade on. Meta Quotes software started about a decade ago, and it gives a trader a choice to choose from the two of its underlying platforms, namely, Meta Trader 4 and Meta Trader 5.

Meta Trader 4

Meta Trader 4 is a very reliable forex trading software that was created by the Meta Quotes because of lack of the software in the forex market. This platform has unique features that aid in the easiness of trading. The features offered by this platform include but not limited to; Limit orders, Pending orders, Multi Charting, More than 50 indicators that can help analyze the trade and so many others. This [platform is very stable and flexible because it has mobile apps. It means you do not need a laptop to monitor your trade if you are trading on this platform. However, the platform is argued the slowest platform in the forex trade by some traders.

The Meta Trader 4 platform has other add on to make it more effective in its work. The Meta Trader 4 platform add on is called the Meta Trader 4 Supreme Edition. If you are using the Meta Trader 4 platform, you download this add on and install it. It will offer you more improved services of the MT4 platform. It makes the click trader feature more flexible.

Meta Trader 5

Meta Trader 5 is a faster trading platform compared to the Meta Trader 4 platforms. This makes it the best trading platform in the forex market. This platforms gives a lot of support to more orders and has more indicators in its features. Unlike in Meta Trader 4, Meta Trader 5 handled vast volumes of transactions. Otherwise, their work is almost the same compared to each other. Meta Trader 5 has more times frames that a trader can view compared to other forex trading platforms. It also can change from the hedging mode to the precise pattern at any time. All these qualities and many more others make the Meta Trader 5 the best platform to trade with.

Just like the Meta Trader 4 supreme Edition Add-on, the Meta Trader4 5 platform also has a Meta Trader 5 Supreme Edition add on. This plugin has more advanced and powerful features than any of the forex trade platforms, therefore, giving it an upper hand as the most robust, stable, suitable and reliable trading platform across the forex market. The Meta Trader Supreme Edition has an inbuilt technical analysis insight. It also has inbuilt trading history analyzer that helps in analysis of the history of all trading currencies before going into the trade. All these features and many more added to the Meta Trader 5 platform, they make it the best platform there is.

C-Trader

This platform is a forex trading platform that was created by spot ware, where this platform has a limit to the third party users. This platform has lesser features than the Meta Trader 4 and 5. It is not so advanced like the other two platforms.

Other forex trade platforms are in use, but the stock traders mostly use some, futures traders, and the active Forex. These platforms include the Ninja Trader, e-signal trading platform, and the ProReal Time trading Platform.

While trading in forex, sometimes you will need a broker to help you in your business for various reasons well preserved by yourself. There are different factors that you will need to consider before choosing your broker. You do not want to choose someone who will make your money disappear in a blink of an eye. Below are the factors to consider;

Security: You have to check out the legitimacy of your broker from a regulatory agency before deciding to trade with him. You cannot give someone your money just because he claims he is real. Be wary of scammers.

Commission Charges: You do not want to choose someone that will take away all your profits as commission. Get a broker you can afford to pay and have some change to keep.

Deposit and Withdrawal Freedom: Get a broker who will allow you to withdraw your money the way you want freely. It is your money, and he should not prohibit you from removing it. He should also allow you to deposit money in the account the way you want.

Trading Platform: Get a broker who has a friendly trading platform. Do not pick a trader just because his charges are low. You should also consider his trading platform flexibility and reliability. If it is a platform that will help you trade well, then go for it. Otherwise, you have the right to turn the broker down if you are dissatisfied with his trading platform.

Excellent Customer Service: Nobody is perfect. Brokers just like you also making faults. The problem comes in when there is no communication. Pick a broker who will communicate in case of anything.

Chapter 3: Fundamental and Technical Analysis

Fundamental Analysis

Fundamental analysis is a financial market analysis method to know the price movements and predict the future outcome of the prices of the asset in the market. Fundamental analysis in forex trading has its focus centered overly on the economy.

The analysis also researches on a variety of factors that affect the forex trade as well as how the elements affect the national currency value. Various factors influence the economy, and theses include interest rates, employment, unemployment, GDP, international trade, and manufacturing industries.

In fundamental forex analysis, the price of the may differ from the value of the same asset in the market. Prices may vary because of various factors, and because of the difference in the price and the value of the asset, different markets underprice or overprice the demands for a short period.

However, the fundamental analysists believe that despite the value of the assets being underpriced, mispriced, or overpriced in the short period, and it always goes back to its original correct price after some time. The main objective of any fundamental forex analyst is to get the right price and value of the asset, compare the two, and finally come up with an opportunity to trade.

Fundamental analysis is very different from technical analysis. Fundamental analysis does not pay a lot of attention to the current price like the technical analysis. The fact is that fundamental analysis is not an excellent analysis tool for intraday traders in forex trading. Forex fundamental analysis has many different theories that try to explain it and make it a suitable analysis tool for forex trading. The most common approach is economic theory. This theory attempts to explain that the price conditions should be exchanged when they are adjusted. It summarizes that this exchange should be done according to the local economic factors.

Major Economic Indicators

The economic data in the market shows the movement of the economy of different countries. A trader who wants to invest should be very keen on commercial change. The major economic indicators show the price movements, comparing it to their values giving the traders opportunities of finding new trading chances to invest and profit.

Inflation

Inflation is the balance between the circulation of money in economic growth and distribution. Each country or market has a set level of which the rise can reach. There is a healthy inflation level and unhealthy inflation level. If the economic growth and money circulation in the market are not maintained, the country or any market is likely to suffer from crippling inflation. The balance between the two brings about a healthy inflation. Every economy works very hard on their economies so that the sound economic level can be maintained.

When inflation is high in any economy, supply and demand are disturbed. Supply gets an advantage because there is more than what is demanded. This high inflation affects the currency negatively. The currency drops. Oppositely, when inflation is low-deflation, there is more demand than supply. During this deflation period, money value rises, and the cost of goods go down in the market. It is a strategy that most economies employ but on a short term basis. If deflation strategy is used long term, it will have adverse effects on the economy. The responsible party will get a hard time stabilizing their economy again.

Gross Domestic Product (GDP)

Gross Domestic Product of a country is the sum of all the monetary value of all goods and services of a given country within a specific time frame. This monetary value of the goods and services must be produced within the borders of that same country. A country's Gross Domestic Product is calculated annually, although there is a possibility of calculating it quarterly depending on the countries policy concerning the GDP calculation.

Gross Domestic Product is the best economic indicator among other economic indicators. Most people think GDP can never be an indicator because it only measures the market value of the goods and services, but they are wrong. From forex fundamental analysis view, when there is an increase in a gross domestic product without an increase in the demand of the products, this constitutes to a weak economy.

Interest Rates

There are different types of interest rates, but the main focus of fundamental forex analysis falls on the nominal and the base interest rates. The central banks of different states set these interest rates. The central bank has to lend money to private banks after creating money. Therefore, the interest amount paid by the private banks on the loans they have acquired from the central bank is called the nominal interest. The nominal interest rate is also known as the base interest rate.

Interest rates balance any economy in the world. It is probably the most reliable economic factor indicator for any forex trader to look at before going into the trade. The interest rates- nominal have a significant influence on the values of the assets, in this case, on the currencies. They also influence other factors like unemployment, manufacturing, investment, and inflation.

Since it is the duty of the central bank control and boost the economy of the country, it makes sure that inflation reaches the country's set level and does not go past that. If it wants to boost the economy of a respective country, it brings down the interest rates. When the nominal interest is down, more private banks will go to the central bank to borrow money while individuals will go to the private banks to borrow money. There will be high production and high consumption correspondently. This act of the central bank will improve the economy of a country but in a short time not a long time.

In as much as interest rates are good at improving the country's economy, it is a poor strategy. The low-interest rates in the markets after a long time will cause over-inflation of cash in the economy and cause an imbalance in this economy. The imbalance caused by this low-interest rates is likely to affect the country for a long time before the economy goes back to normal. Sometimes it paralyzes the country's economy entirely.

However, most of the central banks have a remedy for this inflation. When the economy starts swaying, or after a short period of reducing the interest rates, the central banks increase the scales again. When the interest rates are raised, the money circulating in the market decreases. The private banks will not take loans, and the individuals will not go to the private banks borrow. So when the interest rates start changing, a forex trader should find his opportunity and make an entry or exit in the trade.

A trader should put in mind that the information released on the economic data is critical. He should carefully consider it, with the forex fundamental analysis if he wants to succeed in the forex trade.

Advantages of Fundamental Analysis

- Show the trend of the market price.

- Can be an excellent and reliable indicator, especially when it is combined with the technical analysis. It can work out for long term trades.

Technical Analysis of Forex Trading

When price patterns change from one to another, causing a change of prices in the market, these patterns have a specific way of doing so. When changes in price patterns in markets are studied and mastered to help in the prediction of future price patterns, this is now called the technical analysis. Most traders prefer using technical analysis over fundamental analysis. However, some traders use both the analysis techniques. Technical analysts use a different method to analyze the price patterns in markets. The techniques used include:

Chart Patterns

These are patterns where the prices are drawn on charts inform of graphs. When data is drawn on the graph, there is always a repetitive pattern. This pattern shows the movement of the prices in the forex markets. It shows the strength and the weakness of the trade. Some forex traders use the chart patterns as continuation signals or the reversal signals.

The continuous signals contain, triangle, flag and pennant, channel and cup with the handle while the reversal includes, double top reversal, double bottom reversal, triple top reversal, head and shoulders and so many other. There are three groups of chart patterns that traders use — these chart patterns area the candlestick patterns, the harmonic patterns, and the traditional patterns.

The technical analysts using this chart patterns use horizontal lines, trend lines, and the Fibonacci retracement level to find the signals of the chart patterns. The chart patterns show the strength and weakness of the forex market.

Horizontal Lines

These lines are also called sideways trends. These lines connect the lows and the highs in the variables. In this case the prices on the charts. These lines show the price that is below the support level and above the resistance level.

Trend lines

Trend lines are lines drawn on the chart or the graph to show support or resistance. These trend lines are dependent on the direction in which the prices are going in the forex trade. They are also known as horizontal support and resistance. When analysts are using trend lines in the chart patterns, they can see the increase or decrease in supply and demand.

The traders make up their mind whether to invest or not when this increase or decrease occur. When the prices are going up, it is called an upward trend, and the forex traders can sell. When the prices are going down, it is called a downward trend, and buyers can make their entry in the trade.

Fibonacci Levels

This levels in chart patterns exhume the hidden support and resistance. The support and resistance can be hidden due to the golden ratios. The origin pf Fibonacci is from the mathematical proportion, but it acts like the old support and resistance in the chart patterns when the price levels are laid out. The mathematical proportions used in this method is very different from the highs and the lows on the price charts.

Candlestick Patterns

Forex technical analysts use to find the open, high, and low price levels in the markets (OHL). The prices sought must be of a specific period in the trading session so that a comparison of the trader's behavior during the trade is made against the prices at that particular time. This analysis will help in predicting the future price movement in the forex trade market.

Technical Analysis Indicators

The technical forex analysts use the price action indicator. These indicators include;

The moving average

The moving average indicator shows the averages of prices in a given period. The moving averages display the direction of the market. The moving average helps balance the prices in the market by removing the unwanted prices. This removal helps the trader focus on the trend of the prices in the market. There are four types of the moving averages, namely the exponential moving averages (EMA), simple moving averages (SMA), linear weighted average (LWA), and the smoothed averages.

Bollinger Bands

This indicator is a tool used in technical analysis that comprises of three lines. These lines are plotted positively and negatively but away from the simple moving average of the currency price. These lines are adjustable to the trader's preference. The Bollinger bands help measure the variation degree of prices during the trade. In simpler terms, it measures the volatility of the market in a given period.

Amongst the three lines in the Bollinger, the middle line shows the trend direction of the prices while the upper and lower lines are the volatility lines, also called the volatility bands. The upper and the lower bands are moved above and below the middle band by two standard deviations. This movement of the upper and the lower bands put the price between the two outside lines. This price does not stay here for a long time because it is always moving around the middle line.

The Moving Average Convergence Divergence (MACD)

This price indicator shows the momentum of the market. It shows when the market is doing well or not and the force behind this action. While using this indicator, a signal will always be evident is a market is moving in one direction. The Moving Average

Convergence Divergence indicator belongs to a class of oscillators. Oscillators are technical indicators too and shown separately, below the prices in the charts.

Technical analysis has principles that should be followed during the review.

Principle of Technical analysis

Price Moves according to trends

Technical analyses assume that the prices in the trend move according to the trend patterns. The prices move in a bullish trend, bearish trend, and the sideways trend.

All price movements repeat themselves

The theory in this principle called the Dow Theory assumes that the price of a commodity represents its actual value, and it does not have to look at other factors. The principle claim that the prices in the patterns are repetitive and any future price is likely to be the same as the current price.

Advantages of Technical Analysis

Shows the Trend of the Market

Technical analysis shows the traders direction of the market. They can know the time the downward movement of prices and the upward movement, hence enabling them to make to sell or buy at the appropriate time.

Shows the trader Both Entry and Exit points

Timing is essential to a person trading in the forex. Poor timing will cause significant losses and which will cause the trade to fail. The technical analysis predicts the time for investment for traders. It gives traders the upper hand to know when entering the trade or exit that trade.

Different indicators in technical analysis aids traders get the advantage of knowing investment time early. The candlesticks, moving averages, chart patterns, trend lines, and others indicators help in the calculation of the entry and the exit time in the trade.

Technical Analysis is fast

Technical analysis is fast in giving information about a specific trade. This action makes it quick and reliable to short term traders like the intraday traders who trade in one minute to thirty minutes. In this trade, candlestick patterns are used.

Technical Analysis Gives Adequate Information

Short term traders use technical analysis, swing traders, and long term traders. Enough information is found in the chart patterns, and forex traders can use this information to their advantage. The traders can pursue their trades utilizing this information and get satisfying returns. More details like the trading psychology, market momentum, volatility, support, and resistance is a portion of the vital information that the technical analysis provides.

Technical Analysis is Cheap

Technical analysis of soft wares is cheap. Some soft wares are free offers from different charting software companies, and they can even be downloaded on mobile apps.

Gives an Early signal

The technical signal traders and investor early on when the time is right to invest. It is like a wake-up call to go in or come in or out of the trade. The correct entry or exit time for traders will help them good gains on their trades.

Chapter 4: How to Actually Trade Forex

Forex Trading Technicalities

You first of all need to practice trading with a demo account. As it is with Forex trading, it is not easy to make profits. Practice makes perfect, so you need to do a lot of practice, to acquire many skills of the trade before you actualize it.

Through practice, the demo account gives you to a tune of 100k or 10k free for learning. This is the amount you would never wish to play with on your real account. Through the demo accounts, you will be able to learn issues like placing orders and how it all works as well as placing of stop loss orders.

Paper Trading

Paper trading in actual sense does not entail paper work, but instead it is all about an account simulator. Simulator is the act of trading but with a dummy account for learning and knowledge purposes. So paper-work is all important as you launch into Forex trading.

Before the emergence of simulators, people could use real papers for demonstration. It was until you felt like you were now ready for the real business is when you went in fir the real business.

This back dates to early 1930's where opening of real accounts through brokerages was not easy and cheap either and because of such, you could never wish to do practice on your real account that held your finances.

Why you need a demo account

- On demo account or simulator, you do not need to invest any money either for demonstration purposes however you use virtual money- no risking at all.

- Trading systems can be tested using various trading strategies

- It is easy to learn leveraging

- It more practical and thus real knowledge is acquired that can be applied directly to the market.

Disadvantages

i.   No financial risking is involved therefore you may react uniquely when it comes to reality.

ii.   It is much explorative. You can trade the money that may never be real for you therefore it is imaginary.

Is It Good To Use Demo For Learning?

The answer is definitely yes. This is for anyone that has interest in Forex trading yet new to the system.

As we know well, trading Forex is much of leverage that trading on our own finances. You will be exposed to many financial positions as well as lots. You can open as many lots as you can but, you need to begin with one lot.

The Psychology of Trade

As you gain knowledge, you need to mature to real account for you to realize the difference. You are good to go. The moment you lose money, you will develop some fear.

In this instance, you will be reluctant in position closing for fear of failure of which it happens. On the contrary, when you close a position at a profit, you become greedy. You will tend to close the position at this level yet I could have fetched you more profits.

Yes, you have become emotional. The reason is that, you are now working on reality. You tend to become emotional with this business and end up making impossible decisions instead of following the trading plans.

Emotions if not attended to well; you may end up making wrong decisions only. You need to control them for your survival. This calls for a trading plan. You need to have a very inclusive plan and discipline yourself to adjust to it for your benefit.

Demo Trading as a Learning Method

- Come up with one account from the brokers

- Develop trading strategies and plans to follow

- Work with several position sizes-integrate the position-sizes to the trade. Try different pair of currencies with unique time frames as well

- Put to test you trading plan-try as hard not to lose money for a given time frame.

When you excel on demonstration account,

- Go in for the real account

- Begin with the funds you may not be shocked if lost.

- Use your trading plan to set working goals and not imaginary as with the demo account

- Always begin with small positions first.

If the business seems profitable enough,

- Launch deeper with the increase in sizes of positions.

Chapter 5: Strategies and Forex Trading Tools

We must explore the strategies and tools required for this trade to move on. Trading tools are available on market but they may not be applicable to you al at the same time. For example: oscillators and averages among others.

Most traders make silly mistakes of mixing them all. Every tool on charts acts on different signals. Having many tools on chart will simply confuse you because you will want to work on various signals which is not possible.

The main important point is to learn on how to use a given tool at a time. Working with many signals is good however you may end up blank in your brain. For you to master the game well, try out with few averages with a single oscillator on different parameters.

Which Is The Right Strategy?

There are many strategies in this case that you can follow. For instance, some people would follow a trend on longer-time frame, yet to others, they will prefer to opens several positions as time goes by. The latter is referred to as swing trading.

As for the case of new traders, it could be well if you went in for a strategy that lets you trade on high time-frames. On these high time-frames, you will have time of analyzing the current situation as well as checking other time-frames.

If a good move is established, you may end up profiting much. On lower time frames however, making money may call for leveraging which is a time bomb to new traders on the market.

Invisible Price Action is ever a Common Error

The price is the key speaking concept in this trading strategy. You may add as many indicators as possible with averages however you may end up missing the right price action. This calls for trading on naked charts more often.

Pivot Point

It is a very important trading tool you should consider.

A pivot line is the line ever in the middle. For instance: "R1,R2 and R3", are called resistance lines that are found above the pivot lines whereas "s1,s2 and s3", are support lines usually found below the pivot line on a chart.

More levels are ever calculated in s4's and r4's however, in reality levels 1, 2, 3 are the most calculated. They are evaluated basing on the previous trading periods. They yield to highs, lows as well as close. For example:

One hour pivot points are evaluated on high-low-close of the preceding hour. It is so for four-hour, week, day or even monthly pivots and yearly.

R's and S's are lines that work as price resistance and support concurrently. This implies that prices usually revolve around these lines. In case of an uptrend, if the resistance is hit, there is always a correction back to the pivot lines.

Management of Money and Positions

It is good to consider stop loss orders placements in your trading. They will help you keep your loses at minimal levels in order to destruct your attention from being controlled emotionally.

If you implements these stop loss orders for example, you could be having a series of trades to be lost yet the margin of the loss won the that big. That is, the subsequent trade could be more beneficial.

Lots and Pips

As soon as you develop cold feet in foreign exchange trade, you will be forced to think of lots. A lot is simply the smallest possible trade size or position you can trade in on the Forex market. A lot is directly proportional to the risk expected.

Lot Size is Important

It is good to know the lot size which best suites your position on the financial market and relation to your assets. You will encounter lots of different sizes on the market for you to choose from.

When you trade say 100-pip, such move on a small trade won't be realized as compared with if you traded the same on a large trade-size.

Micro-Lots

Are the smallest-tradable lots that are available with the majority brokers; on the other hand, a macro-lot consists of one thousand units of the currency funding in your account. Assuming that your account is being funded in US dollars, it means that a micro lot is $1,000-worth of the total amount that you wish trade in.

Suppose you are interested in a pair involving dollars, then a single pip will be equated to ten cents. Trading with micro-lots is very beneficial to starters because they limit the risks as you move on with the trade.

Mini-Lots

These existed before the emergence of the micro-lots. If you step up the micro lot by 10, you arrive at mini-lot. That is: 1,000*10=10,000, this is a mini lot. If you are trading with a dollar based currency pairs, then we can say that a single pi could be equated to one dollar ($1).

For starters who would wish to trade with mini-lots, what you require most is a large capital base. A single pip may seem as too small however, there are lots of pips that the market moves within an hour or in a single day. Therefore, if you trade with small amounts, you risk losing much.

Standards Lots

This is different from micro and mini lots. A standard lot is 100 times of the micro lot. In this case 1000*100=$100,000. This is only if your trade is in dollars. In this case, the pip size of the standard lot is equivalent to ten dollars per single pip.

Pip

This is the least sum by value of any pair of currency that can change. For example in a currency combination of US dollar and Euros as EUR/USD, suppose their values move up by a pip, i.e. from: 1.20030 up to 1.20031, the amount has increases by just one pip.

For beginners, it is easy to weigh the level of success or losses on the account in terms of pips other than the real value in dollars.

Generally, the least possible size money being traded in Forex trading for the professionals is what is called lots. For the case of USD related pairs, the lot is $100,000.

This is the least entity of price for any given currency. As you have seen almost all quoted pair have got 5-figures with a decimal point following the first digit. For example: EUR/USD is 1.1234. This indicates that a single pip is equal to the slightest change in the 4th decimal place which is .0001.

Understanding Margin

Every time you come with a new trading account/margin account with brokers, you need to deposit some considerable amount in it. This amount may vary depending on the broker you are investing with. This could go from as small amount as one hundred dollars to one hundred thousand dollars.

Whenever you initiate a trade, there is always a percentage of the balance in your account of that margin account that is put aside and will be used as the initial margin necessity in the upcoming new trade.

Leverage and Leveraging

It is a ratio of capital investment to the needed security deposit. It is also the ability of the trader to take care of huge dollar amounts financial asset using significantly low capital.

It comes in ratios depending on the brokers you are involved with and also the country in which you are trading from. Usually it is in ratios of 500:1 to 2:1 in that order.

All that said and done, we need to embark on how to make money, or money making process in Forex trading. By now, you must be well versed with the technical terminologies as used in the whole of Forex trading and that you are now free to advance your knowledge in other areas comfortably.

Forex trading is much similar to any kind of trade in financial markets for example stocks markets and therefore if you had any prior knowledge of the same, then you stand greater chance sofa learning the trade so easily.

The main agenda of the trade is to trade one currency against the other through exchange with a primary expectation that there will be price changes.

What we mean here is that, you will have high hopes that the currency you bought will have its price go higher than the one which you sold for you make some profit.

Example: let's say that you are interested in trading with the US dollar against Euros. Assuming you bought 10,000 US dollars at a rate of 1.1700 and after like one week you realize that the rates of exchange have gone high like say 1.2600 and that you would wish to dispose the money, then you will earn 900 US dollars.

This can be arithmetically represented as follows: EUR 10,000*1.17=US $11,700 and EUR 10,000*1.126=US $12,600.

Risk Management Concepts

When we talk about Forex trading risks, we mean the challenges that come up in the course of the trade.

These challenges are security threats to the business that may yield to lose.

Forex market offers one of the largest platforms for financial trading with vast markets across the entire globe. There are very many transitions being conducted with large sums of money across the globe.

We are having banking institutions as well as other great organizations and potential individuals exchanging millions to trillions each day each making losses or profits in that order. This comes about as a result in the changes in rates.

As with every market and traders, every participant needs to gain more profits with minimal or no loses at all. However, in every trade where there is a great expectation of returns, there must be great risks involved.

In order to minimize losses, every investor is required to put in place some risk management guidelines or precautions.

You need to be aware of the potential risks and how to manage them suppose they arise in the course of trading. One thing that we need to understand is that there is no way you can avoid inevitable in the case of risk and potential loses.

1. Do not risk more than what you can afford to lose

This is a common mistake as with Forex traders and more especially to the beginners who are still very excited with the venture. Because of the vulnerability of the Forex markets, you invest what you feel you cannot be frustrated in case of a loss.

When you invest lots of money to this kind of trade and especially as a beginner, you risk and place yourself in a more vulnerable state of risks from the market.

Anything can happen on to the Forex market. Any slight news on currencies can affect the rate of currencies and therefore lead to loses.

2. Emotional Management

It will be well for every Forex trader to have a mechanism of controlling his emotions else, it can be so hard to patiently persist until you reach your goals. Forex markets are so volatile. Volatility is the most common and threatening risk sin this trade set up.

If you are stubborn, you may never stand to achieve anything in this kind of trade. You may wait for so long to exit just one position. It is so good to exit positions whether there are profits or not. It is better to move away with a small loss than wait to lose it all.

The more you keep on waiting, you end losing much capital. When you opt out, you need to be very patient for opportunities to crop before joining the trail again.

3. Create and Follow a Trading Plan

Due to volatility in this business, it is good to come up with a master plan that will guide you in every possible move that you intent to make. As such you need to stick to it carefully to avoid weak and premature decisions that are often made as a result of emotions.

There are high levels of risks in this industry that makes it not suitable to all kinds of investors. Mistakes should be limited as you major on with the trade. More attention is required in the creation of the trading plan. This can be equated to the investment for your future profitability.

You can achieve all these with the few selected tips as outlined below:

- Remember that money values change with time and therefore, there are many individuals, firms and other organizations that are affected globally.

- The changes in the exchange rates do affect money channels, financial assets and liabilities

You can only realize this if you engage small-amounts of finances as capital to your business and then monitor closely the trends of the markets.

4. *Spending More Than You Earn*

You cannot spend more than what you earn in reality. However, this is happening in greater situations in that, you exhaust whatever you have earned and go in for loans or credit in order to fulfill your desires with a hope off paying for it future.

5. *Lack Of Insurance to Your Money*

This is very dangerous in cases of damages or sickness. You will be required to dig deep into your pockets to solve the pending case, yet if you had invested in an insurance plan, it could take care of such risks without your struggle.

It is quite important to invest part of your income in an insurance cover so that some future unknown risks can be alleviated or handled minus your spending.

6. *Lack of Emergency Funds*

Lack of a contingency fund is a common mistake that people ever commit yet this is the money or resource that can get you out of a distress whenever you expect or find yourself in one.

There is a belief that your monthly income will take care of everything in the family however, that is not the true. Contingencies are inevitable to all and as such you need to have separate account put aside to cater for the unexpected as soon as it occurs.

Chapter 6: Further Information on Forex Trading

Risk/Ratio reward

It is so good to maintain you risk: reward ratio at 1:3 or 1:2. In this case, the trader could be willing to place say; $2/share but hopes for $4/share in the ratios 1:2 or $6 thus 1:3 respectively. If the ratio of the risk to the reward is say; 1:1, no business is initiated because it won't be of any worth.

Good and experienced traders looking for greater opportunities are able to identify where to put stops at every interval. They do not enter trades blindly to begin fumbling with what next. They are already equipped with the knowledge on how to place the stop loses.

When Stop-Losses Are Suitable?

The time when you place your orders, is the right time possible to place the stops. This should be in your mind as early as possible. While placing your orders, you should also consider placing the stop orders as well right away.

When you delay placing of stop loss, you may be tempted to do so when it is too late therefore doing it emotionally. This yield to poor results or loses at most.

Where to Set Stop Loss

There is a procedure to follow when setting stop losses. We will review that briefly, but as for now let's take some time and explore the common mistakes that people do as far as stop losses are concerned.

Tight stop losses

When you place your stop too-tight, means that you may be stopped at your very greater move. Due to the volatility of the markets today, you may risk being stopped too soon as your stop is too close. This ever occurs to those traders who fear losing many finances.

The nature of stop loss is its nearness to entry point and therefore if triggered, there will be a minimized loss on its account. The challenge here is the fact that tight stops are triggered too soon and quite often. If this happens, many small loses will be found on your account which May accrue to big sums.

Wide stop losses

There is no one who likes being send out of trading. You may have a stop loss put so wide in order to avoid being stopped out of trading. They fear being caught as a result of correction or stop-hunting. Such stops are rare however if found to be triggered, the loss is enormous.

As you invest in trending markets, you only initiate trades when there is a trend else not. In the case of upward- trending there are higher-highs as well as higher-lows as it is on charts.

When the trends are strong and healthy, it is easy to notice the trends via the prices. If the trend is affected, the prices do not go high these calls for a corrective measure to be taken.

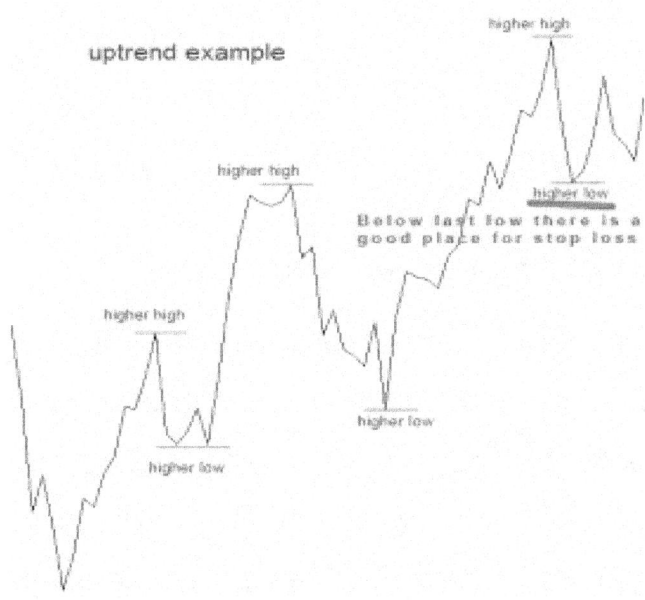

Stop loss being set below the last low.

Provides with the relevant information, it is possible to place a stop under the last low assuming that you are holding a long position. In this case, if there is a healthy trend then you need to grab big sums. However, if the trend becomes weak, chances are that you may bounce out. So it is very important since the prices may go down beyond your stop-loss.

In the event of a down trend, you aim at placing your stop loss higher than the previous high as shown in the figure below:

A Stop Loss Being Placed In Down-Trend

We need to consider the logic in this example. Suppose the downtrend price breaks above the preceding high, chances are that buyers are working hard to overtake the trade by controlling the parameters. You may not be willing to become short as such; you will wish to close-down your position as you venture in to others.

Increasing Stop Loss

Raising stop loss is every easy. You need to do that at the point of setting up the trade. Recall that you may be locked out too soon or it may end up as you projected. The question that you need to ask yourself is that how do you behave in the case of profit realization?

It may even turn upside down and activate the stop-loss whereby whatever was to be profitable, turn out to be a potential loss. It could happen with anyone if you are not very careful.

If your trade is profitable, I means that your stop loss in being raised to the entry-point. In this case, price change does not affect your current position either and you do no stand to lose anything.

You don't raise your stop loss as soon as the trade becomes more profitable, instead it is better to wait for the price to be like twice as compared to the entry point as it will be with the stop loss.

For instance: If at the entry point, the price of a position was 20 yet the stop set to 28, the stop loss could be raised to 30 when the prices go up to 34.

This is to say; at the beginning, the stop-loss was $2 below the entry point and as soon as the entry position raised its position by twice the stop loss to 34, then the stop is increased by 2.

As the prices go up, it is good to raise your stop loss in order to take care of the profits. Even though the prices fall below target, you are still sure of some profits. This is referred to as Trailing-Trade simply because the stop-loss is basically chasing after the prices.

Orders

An order signifies to the way someone enters and exits the trade. There are a number of orders which are placed on foreign exchange markets. Recall every broker has got different types of orders that he can place in Forex markets.

Here are some of the orders as discussed in detail for your consideration.

Market orders

This is an order to either buy or sell at the best price available on the market. For instance: Suppose the bid price for the pair EUR/USD stands at 1.2240 yet the ask price stands at 1.2242, assume you wanted to purchase the pair, be sure of buying it at a price 1.2242.

When you click the buy option on the trading platform, be sure your choice will be effected instantly and that you will have executed the order.

Remember that, depending on the nature of the market trends, you may click on that price but at the end you find that the price at which the order was executed was different due to fluctuation.

Limit-Entry Order

This is an order that is placed on sell-above the market or buy-below the market at a given price. For instance: in EUR/USD assuming that it is trading at 1.2040, and that you are hoping to go short or sell off when the price goes to 1.2060.

There are potentially two ways of doing this exercise. You can decide to remain calm at your computer as you wait for the prices to reach the expectation then click and initiate the selling or rather set the sell limit order at this price as you go on with other issues.

As soon as the price hits the target thus 1.2060, the trading platform will execute the trade in this case, the sell-order at the best-price available. This order type is the one to be used whenever you hope that the prices will turn out to hit your expectation.

On the other hand, when you use a limit order for buying at a price slightly lower than the market-price, the order shall be executed when the prices equal to or even lower than the expected price value.

A limit-order to sell higher than the market-price, shall be affected when the price is either equal or slightly higher than the specified price value.

A stop-Entry Order

You place a stop-entry order so as to either buy above or sell below the markets at a given price value.

For instance: using GBP/USD and that it is trading at 1.5055 and that it is increasing. If the prices continue to escalate, you are sure of hitting 1.5065.

In this case, there are measures you can take such as stay awake at your system to buy at market as soon as it hits 1.5065 or else initiate the stop-entry order at exactly 1.5060 as you go on with other issues.

Stop-loss Order

This is an order that is used in Forex trading to limit loses whenever the prices shift unmanageable levels. In the case of a long-position, you execute sell stop else if you are in a short one, you execute the buy stop orders respectively.

There is one thing that you need to understand about the uniqueness of this type of order. As opposed to other orders, this one will still take effect to the level when the position is liquidated or else you will be forced to cancel it.

For instance: you decide to 'go-long' with EUR/USD at 1.2260. In order to lower the risk of loses; you decide to set up your order at 1.2240.

In this case of incorrect prediction and that the prices drop to 1.2240 other than going higher, the execution of the sell order at that level shall be affected automatically. You will be able to close out but with a twenty pip loss. Too bad!

We can say that stop loses are very essential for those who have no time to spend at their computers to monitor the shifts in the trends through the day with the fear of losing out of the trade.

What you need to do, is to set the stop-loss order for all or any open-position so that you engage in any other relevant errands that you have. One advantage of the stop-loss orders is that it's not quite involving and that it saves the investor's time.

The other advantage is that you can get involved in different businesses at the same time and still expect to make big margins of profits. It is said to be one of the very essential orders that any Forex trader needs to invest his time in learning how it works.

A Trailing-Stop Order

This type of order is entirely associated with the trade which moves with price fluctuations. Assume that you have shorted USD/JPY at 90.60 using a trailing-stop of 20-pips. What this implies is that the stop-loss order will be at $90.80. Suppose the prices go down to $90.40 it means that the trailing-stop will definitely shift to 90.60.

One thing which you need to remember here is that the trailing-stop will settle at the new price index. It cannot grow wide even if the market rises above your control.

As in the above example where there is 20-pip trailing stop, suppose the trading pair shifted to 90.20, then automatically, the trailing stop would shift to 90.40. This means that there will be a lock of about $20 as the profit.

As long as the price on market hit the trailing-stop, automatically, a market order will be executed for the closure of the position when the price is still good. This will automatically lea to profits in that event.

Weird Orders

As the name suggest, these are orders that do not yield anything and do not make sense in any way whatsoever. In most occasions, they do not exist or if they do, then they are lees important and likable by anyone on the Forex market. It is as good as you never had an order before.

Consider someone in a restaurant making f breakfast and lunch and dinner with some deserts at the same time. He becomes vague, that is the same case as with weird orders.

GTC-Good 'Till Cancelled

This is a type of order that is open in market as long as you have not cancelled it. Remember that your broker cannot cancel your order at all costs. You must take it into consideration of all the orders that are active.

When you schedule orders, you have to make sure that they are cancelled otherwise you face the consequences.

GFD-Good for the Day Orders

This order also will be active as long as the trading day is still on. Recall that Forex business or market is on a

24-hour platform, so we mean the time of closure of business in the United States which is 5pm EST.

OCO-One Cancel the-Other

This consists of two or more orders as entry and a stop-loss order. You will find that two different orders of different features are placed one above as the other is below the current prices. As one of the orders gets executed, the pending one definitely gets nullified.

For example: assume EUR/USD is 1.2030. Perhaps you are willing to purchase at say 1.2085 above the resistance-level with a hope that the prices will go down even below 1.2075.

In this example as above, the explanation is that, you expect the buy ordered to be triggered as soon as the price reaches 1.2085 and that if it goes down, the sell order will be cancelled at 1-2075.

OTO- One Triggers the Other

This is the exact opposite of the OCO. This type of order is only executed after the execution of the parent order. It is only set with an intention of setting profit-taking with stop-losses in advance long before you begin the exercise of trading.

For instance: Suppose USD/CHF is at 1.1000 and you have trust that it will rise to 1.1100, what happens here is that, it will go backwards only to reach at 1.900.

The challenge here is that you may wait for an entire week until you lose hope. For you to succeed as you won't be closer to monitor the trends and the entire changes, you need to set the order called the sell-limit at 1.1000 and in addition to that place a relative buy-limit at 1.900, and for that matter put a stop loss order a1.1100.

Conclusion

Forex traders ever need all these types of orders for them to execute their businesses very well.

You need to go slow with the feature of the Forex trading for you achieve the most of the business. If you are not yet there, for whatever reasons, don't you ever worry, slow but sure you will be there.

There are a few basics that you need to observe:

- Ensure you understand well and are free with your choice of broker's entry orders and its systems before going in for trade.

- Ensure you check out with your broker for secluded information on orders to ascertain if rollover fee in inclusive to positions held for longer periods than a day.

- The best trading strategy is to ensure your ordering rules are kept as easy as 1, 2, and 3 respectively.

- Only venture in the trading with real money if all the trading basics are at your fingertips and that you are very familiar with the trading platform that you wish to use for the business.

More Understanding on Pips

As we had seen and defined before, a pip is simply a unit that indicates the change in values of two currencies. For instance if you are trading with the pair of EUR/USD and that the values move form say 1.2000 to 1.2010, the change in terms of numerical figure thus .0010 is what refer to as 10 pips.

In brief, a pip is simply the last decimal place on quoted price. It is quite unrealistic to ever imagine that you require a certain number of pips per day. What you need to do is to lay your focus keenly on the trading strategies.

You also need to consider limiting the use of leverage in trade if you ever imagine of getting any better returns over time.

In many cases however much it is not advisable to consider the number of pips per day, you will find that there are those of which would lay much of their focus on the number of pips per day.

Others go ahead looking for strategies which call for a certain number of pips per day. There are many controversies that come up with such strategies and such impractical objectives.

We need to answer this question and go ahead to teach you the best approach working with pips bearing in mind the fluctuations in the market that may affect pips and their trends and how to replace all these with a better strategy.

How Many Pips do Professionals Make?

Professionals never work with a specific number of pips per day on their minds. The fact that markets are very volatile and thus quite unpredictable makes them eliminate the number of pips as targets for the day.

Pips per day vary depending on some factors such as the strategy employed and the set goals by the traders themselves.

There are strategies which aim at smaller yet frequent returns on a series of trades. We call this scalping and others go for strategies which target big returns as they invest on long term periods. We refer this to as position trading.

Setting the Number of Daily Pips Is Unrealistic

It is very true that not all trades conducted produce positive outcome. If you put your focus on measuring the number of pips that you expect or achieve per day is wasting your time and preparing for a big fail.

Daily pip targets cannot be effective with a reason that it supports bias by trading most when the trading strategy isn't very effective hence trading low during effective moments of the trading strategy. As you can see, this is the entire opposite of the expectations.

For instance, suppose trader x, obtains a certain specific pips in the course of the day after placing in a certain number of trades, he will tend to close the positions not imagining of the possible positive outcomes of the subsequent trades that he could have invested in.

Put Your Focus on the Winning Strategy Other Than Pips

It is better for any trader to consider any controllable aspects of the trade other than putting your focus on the unrealistic number of pips per day. You need to follow a working strategy and avoid emotions. This alone can make you successful in your trade.

Avoid imaginary things and fantasies for they are the key contributors of failure in Forex trading.

Chapter 7: Strategies for Beginners

There are many different ways that people run their businesses ranging from the traditional means to more sophisticated means.

The most important aspect in every successful business however, and more especially in Forex trading, is the selection of the most assorted strategies to be applied in different conditions.

Those who have followed entirely one system of trade have found out that it won't offer solutions to the ever changing technology and complexity of the market demands for Forex trade.

It is important for every single trader to have the knowledge and skills of challenging the market circumstances of which is not very easy. It demands for a deep knowledge and revelation of the economics.

In this topic we are going to provide you with the necessary but simple strategies that if applied can lead to a successful Forex business. Recall: these strategies are friendly for the novice traders who would wish to step up their knowledge and skills.

There are various ways in which these trading strategies can be classified. We will consider the basic classifications.

Analysis-Based Trading Strategies

i.   Technical Analysis

As the names suggests, 'analysis', this method focuses primarily on the evaluation of the market trends through charts as a means of predicting the to-be price trends of the market.

In this method, an evaluation of assets is done basing on statistics and past analysis of market actions like the then volumes and the past prices.

Technical analysis is not done with a primary objective of weighing the underlying value of assets; instead, charts with other measuring tools are used to define the patterns that are helpful in future forecast in market actions.

It is believed that the market's future performance is easily determined by the past trends in its performance.

ii.   Trend Trading

In technical analysis, a trend is a very critical aspect. The tools used in this type of analysis, have a common motive which is simply to determine trends of the market. Therefore to trend is to move; in this context it means the way the market is moving.

As we know, fore market is a wavy and zigzag motion that represents the successive trails that define clearly troughs and peaks which are sometimes called lows and highs'?

Depending on the available trends of the lows and highs, it is possible for a trader to define the nature of the market type.

Other than the popular notion of the highs and lows, there is yet another format of the trends in Forex trading called: uptrend/downtrend and sideways trend.

iii.   *Support and Resistance*

It is quite imperative to know the meaning of the horizontal level before defining the support and resistance strategy. This is the level in the price signifying market support of resistance. In technical analysis, resistance and support as used refer to the lows or highs in prices in that order.

Support in this case refers to an area on a chart which shows that the interest in buying is stronger than the selling force.

This is revealed though successive troughs. On the other hand, resistance level, as represented on the chart refers to an area where the buying force is outweighed by the selling concern.

iv.   Range Trading

It is also referred to as channel trading. This signifies the absence market direction that may be associated with lack of trends. It is used to identify the movement in the prices of currencies within the channels of which it is tasked to establish the range in the movements.

It can be achieved by linking sets of lows and highs to the horizontal-trend line. This is to say that the trader is tasked to establish the resistance and support levels with the area in the midst which we refer to as trading-range.

v.   Technical Indicators

When we talk of the technical indicators in reference to Forex trade, we simply refer to the calculations that are inclined to the volume and the price of a given security.

When used, they are meant to corroborate quality and trend in the chart patterns as well enable traders to identify sell and buy signals altogether. These indicators in technical analysis can create sell and buy signals via divergence as well as crossovers.

Whenever the prices go across the moving-average, crossovers are seen however, divergence occurs only if the indicator and the price trends both move in different and opposite directions implying that there is a weakening in the price-trend.

vi.   Forex Charts

In Technical analysis, we refer to a chart as a representation of the shifts in prices within a given time frame graphically. It reveals the movement in the security price over a period of time.

Different charts can be applied in search of diversified information and the skills and knowledge of the researcher. There are several types of charts available for your review such as: point and figure, candlestick, line-chart as well as bar charts.

vii.   Forex volume

Forex volume indicates the total securities by number, traded in a certain time interval. The higher the volume, the higher the level of pressure; this is as indicated by chart specialists.

They can easily define the downward or the upward shifts in volume by observing the volume bars on the lower side of the charts. When a price movement is accompanied with a high volume, it becomes more valuable than if it is accompanied by low volumes.

viii.   Multiple Time-Frame Analysis

Security price must be tracked over a period and in a unique time frame. This is so because a security price will tend to go through a series or time frames and therefore analysts need to review several time frames so that they establish the security's trade cycle.

Trading-Style Based Strategies

This is yet another technique which offers a different way of classifying the trading styles. Through trading styles, trading strategies can be created which could include but not limited to buy-and-hold strategy, portfolio trading, trading algorithm, order and carry trades,

It is entirely dependent on your level of understanding, power and your weaknesses that determines the strategies that you will apply. Everyone needs a trading strategy which best suits his desires according to his ability to apply it.

There is no single ever trading style that one must apply whenever he wants to trade because, what suits one person may not suit you and your needs.

i. Day Trading

This is the act holding a position as well as disposing it off the very same day. This implies that, this type of person does not hold as security for more than a day. There are several strategies that are applied in day trading: fading, momentum, scalping as well as pivot trading.

You have the right if only you have the ability of conducting more than one type of trade in a single day as long as you do not hold a position for more than one day. This means than before the closure of the market, you must have liquidated all your open positions.

There is a challenge in this day trading in that, if you cling on a position for so long, the chances of losing it go high. Based on whatever style you are using, the targets in the price may vary.

a. Scalping Strategy

This is characterized by short and quick operations and is applied mainly to achieve vast returns on small price variations. Scalpers are able to initiate over 200 trades per day with an intention of making good profits on small shifts in price levels.

b. Fading strategy

Fading in this case refers to a trade that is initiated against trends. When the trend shifts upwards, faders do sell hoping that there will be a price drop-down; similarly, they may buy as the prices go up.

They buy when the price is escalating and sell when the prices are coming down a notion called fading. It is very contrary to other trends and also to nature of business.

The trade is usually against the usual trends with reasons such as: the buyers at hand may be risking, the securities are usually over purchased as well as the earlier may be set for profits.

c. Daily-Pivot Trading

Currencies are very volatile and as such, traders may wish to capitalize on that to make profits. This is exactly the case with pivot strategy.

A turning point same as the pivot point is a very critical yet unique pointer obtained through the computation of the statistical average of the low, high as well as closing-prices of currency-pairs.

The secret to this strategy lies in the aspect of purchasing securities at their lowest prices and selling them of at their best prices in the course of the day.

Mathematically it could be represented as follows: [pivot point= (previous close + previous low + previous high)/3]

d. Momentum Strategy

This is characterized by defining the strongest position that will end up trading highest. In this case, the trader may drop the currency with signs of dropping in price and go for that currency that has positive signs of going up through the day.

A momentum trader has got several indicators which help him detect the trends in the securities before he make his decisions called momentum-oscillators. Such a trader will tend to invest deeply to news feeds which he entirely depends on for price predetermination and decision making.

e. Buy & Hold Strategy

In this case, a position is bought and held for quite long before being sold so that the prices escalate even if it takes long. Whoever does this has no business with the short term price changes as well as indications.

However this type of strategy best suits the stock traders.

In this case, technical analysis becomes invalid because trader here is a passive investor who has no rush in determining the market trends of the stocks and securities.

Order-Types Trading Strategies

Trading on order will help the trader to join or move out of a position at the very right time by use of various orders which include but not limited to market, pending limit, stop-loss, and stop as well as other orders

At this particular moment, most advanced platforms are fitted with different kinds of orders for trading that are not the common buy/sell buttons. Every order type signifies a certain strategy. You must have the knowledge of how and perhaps when to handle orders before you can use them effectively.

The following are trader orders that can be applied by traders.

- Market order- is put to enable the trader to buy/sell at the ripe price.

- Pending order-enable traders to buy/sell at previously set prices.

- Limit order-guides the trader to buy/sell assets at specific price levels.

- Stop-loss order-is placed to lower a trade risk.

Algorithmic Based Strategy

This is as well referred to as 'automated' Forex trade. There is software designed to help in predetermination of times for purchasing and selling of the securities. This software operates on signals from draw from the technical analysis.

To trade in this strategy, you need to issue instructions over the kind of signals that you would wish to search for and its subsequent interpretation. This is an example of a high trading platform which comes with other supportive platforms for trading.

Examples of this kind of trading platforms include: meta-Trade 4 and Net-TradeX which we will discuss in details in the chapters to come. However, Net-TradeX is a platform for trading whereby other than its normal functionalities, presents automated-trading through its advisors.

This is referred to as secondary-platform that yields automatic trading and further sophisticates its processes through a language called: "Net-TradeX language."

It goes ahead to provide room for some trading operations traditionally for example; to open and to close a position to place orders as well as use of the technical tools for analysis purposes.

Meta-Trader 4 similarly is a trading platform which makes it possible for execution of algorithmic trade via an incorporated program-language "MQL4". It is in this type of platform where traders can come up with called-Advisors, trading–robots with indicators of their own. All acts of making advisors which include: to debug, to test, to optimize and to compile the program are all done and made active through the meta-Trader 4 editor.

Robots are made in this case to take away the emotional concept of the traders which in most cases hinders the free and competent engagement in the trade across the platforms. Emotions have and supply negative attitude to the traders especially when there is a hope for a loss.

Chapter 8: Money Management and Psychology

Money is a medium of exchange and a basic need for business. All of us need money. The amount of money needed by each one of us is what is left as a challenge to us because of our varied needs.

Every one of us does something with the objective of earning money. The challenge comes in the spending of the earned money. There are many ways in which people spend their finances which sometimes leave them worse than when they had nothing.

In this chapter, we are going to explore the various techniques need to applied in managing of your money and the psychology of money to most people. We will also explore the challenges that face people as a result of lack of money management.

We will be traversing through the different mindsets in the context of money. We will also look at money moments and how to reach the mindsets.

Mindsets are very important to financials because the affect how we plan, develop and market the upcoming financial services. There are four basic mindsets which are believed to be most universal.

Mindsets largely affect the way we conceive plan and effect the market for our future finances. When we talk about money moments, we simply come up with few questions to ponder:

- When does someone think of money matters?

- In what context do you think about it?

- How best do you trouble yourself thinking about money?

Another question that seems to be very general but relevant is that: as you think about money, where is your bank at that particular moment?

Most people have at least four different modes of dealing with money such as:

- Managing it- you are your own decision maker on how to use your money.

- Tracking it-being keen to observe the incomes and expenses and savings as well.

- Acquiring the money –getting money by working and other financial deals and,

- Spending what they have- using your money to get the best out of it.

All these summed up gives an insight on the bond between money and people and possibly their relationship with banks.

Knowing people's mindsets enables you to determine the way people earn money, how they spend it and perhaps how they need to invest it or save at the current ages mindless of the financial strength of the people.

The Power of a Mindset

It is important to know how people spend and save their fiancés, this will help in defining a problem that can eventually yield to a long lasting solution in terms of financial management and empowerment is concerned.

We have achievers mindsets, balancers mindsets, experiences mindsets as well as explorer's mindsets.

As with achievers mindsets, people associate with budgeting for proper reasons. It enables them to be in full control of their future. On the other hand, balancers define success through looking for great deals in transactions, making most out of the deals as they remain tuned to their plans without worrying.

Experiencers take success as living well at the current moment. They only find ways of how they can spend their income as they remain optimistic of their future. Finally the explorers will tend to save more money and perform some tradeoff in order to remain in tune with happy lives and comfort.

Achievers

Achievers however go an extra mile to invest in their future more than their current lives. They feel so vivid with their future goals. They will want to adore their future more by coming up with wiser financial decisions that will enable them invest for the future.

As long as they have a good track record of their future investments, they have no problem with the current situations.

- Achievers will tend to plan ahead and monitor their behaviors towards finances

- They have got well set financial rules that govern their expenditure. They constantly review their future goals against their resources

- They are fond of adjusting budgets to suit their future investment.

- They will ever look for relevant information to guide them on how best to achieve their goals.

Financial Psychology

Whenever it comes to money matters, nobody is actually rational. Sometimes we do not follow up to ensure that we save anything small at the time of our pay even if we so desire to. It is very clear that we need a financial plan even though we do not want be involved in its creation and on the greater side, it never matures.

We tend to spend recklessly lots of money or go ahead to spend too little but under pressure. In the long run, our financial behaviors return a lot of shame to us. No one can avoid money in our plans; we have an intimate relationship with our money.

Such relationships evolve and may affect our lifestyles and subsequently dictate our future. There is a psychology revolving around our financial lives that we need to understand as outlined below:

Finance and emotions

Emotions pose as great threat to financial matters in our lives. We have a feeling of fear, shame, self-guilt and envy. These are just but examples of emotions that can be tied to your financial thinking which need to be taken good care of because left like that, they may kill the rational way of thinking and act as blocks to your actions.

Is there anything to be afraid of? Yes they are however; you need to establish the nature of the fear. Most emotions come in when you feel that what you have won't be enough, you may tend to fear looking foolish, or perhaps the fear of being humiliated.

You may be guilty based on the source of your finances and a how much you have over your friends, at the same time you may become shameful to a level of doing what you never purposed to do with your finances. Take an example of shameful scenarios below:

  a. Lack of enough finances

  b. Financial excuses

  c. Lack of proper budgeting that attracts inevitable

  d. Being ignorant of the basics

  e. Over spending

- Financial anxiety/avoidance

- You can run away from neither your past nor your family at larger.

Mental Health & Illness

This is yet another factor that may contribute to financial misappropriation. In America, there is a great problem related to mental health which can Course a lifelong damage to people. There are effects associated with alcohol such as depression can have a negative effect on you financials.

When under the influence of drugs or alcohol leads to inconsistent judgment, lack of financial attention and can end up jeopardizing your employment and forms of secrecy.

Family & Childhood-Influences

A Psychology of money is found in every household or calls it family. In this relation, who handles the money, how, when, where are some of the key issues that will be found in most families. In addition, there are stories relating to money matters that exist in every family with a clear tracking and can be used as an identity.

It could be that a business opportunity was missed out by the great grandfather, which led to the downfall of the family and any related stories.

Money Mistakes That Need To Be Avoided

As we all know that financial markets are never forgiving. Whenever you commit a felony, it is you to face the consequences because; few are choices that can lead you to a corrective mechanism. At the end of the day, the repercussion could end you up in hot soup of distress.

There are several financial felonies which people make and are affected negatively by them. If they are well take care of them one will have financial freedom.

1. Lack of emergency account

Lack of a contingency account is a common mistake that people ever commit yet this is the money or resource that can get you out of a distress whenever you expect or find yourself in one.

There is a notion that our monthly income will take care of everything in the family however that is not the case. Emergencies are inevitable to all and as such you need to have separate account put aside to cater for the unexpected as soon as it happens.

We have sudden circumstances such as job loss prior to sufficiency in terms of finances could lead you a financial distress. It is therefore good to have a financial plan that can help you have emergency funds that can take you through nine to twelve months prior to your stabilization.

2. First Spend/Save Later

Spending is easier than saving and as such most people tend to save whatever remains after a thorough expense. Spending is like investing for today alone and thus putting your future at higher risk.

It is therefore advisable to save first and then spent what is left. This makes your future goals very perfectly live and being sure of your retirement as well.

3. Saving Money Instead Of Investing

It is easier to keep money idle than in vets in a productive venture. However, money kept idle loses its value over a period of time due to inflation and other factors.

4. Lack Of Proper Planning For Taxes

Everyone must give tax for whatever income you get. If you do not plan for your taxes very well, you might regret at a later stage. It is good to pay the tax well for your ventures and property in order to save and or invest the remaining amount well.

5. Ignoring That Retirement Planning Is Vital

People assume that since retirement age is an issue for discussion, they fail to plan for their retirement. You will find that, in today's economy, most people are going in for early retirement which might leave you without finances suppose it happens to you.

It is therefore very nice to plan for your retirement as early as possible so that if it happens prior to your knowledge, it does not find you as a shock in your later stage of life.

6. Spending More Than Your Income

You cannot spend more than what you earn in reality. However, this is happening in greater situations in that, you exhaust whatever you have earned and go in for loans or credit in order to fulfill your desires with a hope off paying for it future.

7. Lack of enough insurance cover

This is very dangerous in cases of damages or sickness. You will be required to dig deep into your pockets to solve the pending case, yet if you had invested in an insurance plan, it could take care of such risks without your struggle.

It is quite important to invest part of your income in an insurance cover so that some future unknown risks can be alleviated or handled minus your spending.

8. Having A Copy Of Where Your Funds Go To

As it has been from before, one needs to spend his own finances as he earned it. But you will find out that sometimes you do not understand how your money is being spend until when you check out with your bank through a bank statement is when you realize how your money have been spend.

Therefore, it I good to start with analyzing your statement for about a three months in order to find the trend of your earnings and as such be able to budget for your expenses.

9. Living pay slip to pay slip

This actually could a big drawback to any individual especially at this period where the rate of un-employment is on the rise. It is good to have a reservoir of finances that can take you and your families through a period of eight to twelve months that can take care of your expenses suppose something happens and you lose your job or your paycheck.

10. Receiving A Big Tax Return At The End Of The Year

This is a case where you have a lot of money being held by the taxing or loan agents and they opt to give it back to you at once. If this proves to be your best way of saving then, you are better-off than nothing.

This could not be the best way to save your money because you lose the ability of gaining interest on your savings as well you risk losing the whole amount in case of an emergency.

Chapter 9: How to Make Money in Forex

The primary objective for every Forex trader is to make money. However, one should understand that Forex trading is not a cheap means to getting rich or we can say that it is not a short cut to success.

Let us support these with a few points below:

- *Is A Skill That Is Learned Over A Period Of Time*

Only skilled traders make money here, in addition, however much you are skilled, you cannot achieve success in an overnight. It is not a piece of cornflake as you may wish to believe, because if it were the case, every trader in this business could be a rich man.

Even experts encounter loses periodically because there is no trick to the business. It needs a lot of experience and practice in order to major in it. First of all, you need to gain knowledge and put it into practice via a demo account and master it well.

- *Every Expert Loses Money On Some Trades*

Approximately 90% of Forex traders have lost money at a certain interval in the business. This could have been as a result of poor or lack of proper planning, lack of proper training, lack of proper discipline, lack of a trading edge or simply because of poor or lack of proper money management skills.

- *Forex Trading Is Not For The Poor*

It is as simple and clear as it is. The mini account should have to a tune of $10,000 as trading capital before you join the business. Does it sound imaginary, yes, that is the reality. You cannot begin with few coins in your account and dream of being the next millionaire.

Forex market is known for its speculation capacities because of its robustness, liquidity as well as the nature of currencies movement in powerful trends. Another aspect is the number of traders who make a killing has been limited to few individuals.

Those individuals who make gigantic earnings are the one who invest without paying attention to the risk factors in the business.

It is well now that we are aware of the gimmicks of the business, it is a good to go ahead and identify some of the mostly used terminologies in Forex trading that we shall be referring to hare and there.

Major & Minor Currencies

Major currencies refer to those currencies that are ever frequently being traded in and that are very liquid and volatile on the market. There are at least eight currencies in this category namely: EUR, USD, GBP, JPY, CAD, NZD, CHF and AUD. As opposed to this, any other currency on the market is what is called the minor currency.

Base-Currency

In any pair of the trading currencies, the first currency is what we refer to as the base currency. For example EUR/USD, in this case the base currency is the EUR. This implies the base currency's is quoted against the other currency. For instance: if the USD/EUR rate is 1.12300, this means that 1 USD is worth EUR 1.12300

Note: In foreign exchange market, it is the U.S. dollar which is always quoted as the base-currency. This indicates that quotations are ever expressed in terms of one US dollar against the other currency stated in the pair.

Quote-Currency

This is the second in any pair of the quoted currency. It is also called the Pip currency, which signifies the loss or unachieved profit that is always presented here.

Pip

This is the least entity of price for any given currency. As you have seen almost all quoted pair have got 5-figures with a decimal point following the first digit. For example: EUR/USD is 1.1234. This indicates that a single pip is equal to the slightest change in the 4th decimal place which is .0001.

Bid Price

Bid price actually is that price where the currency pair on the market is expected to be bought at. It is at this price that the base currency I sold off by the traders, the currency indicated on the left side of the quote.

Ask Price

The opposite of bid price: This is that where the Forex market is set to give out any currency pair. You are able to buy the base currency at this very price. This is always shown on the left side of the quoted currency.

Bid/Ask Spread

When you hear of a spread, what comes in to your mind should be the difference and in this case, it is that difference of the Ask and Bid prices.

Cross Currency

This is a currency quote where neither of the quoted currencies is in US dollars. This comes with very unique yet high price characteristics which mean that the trader has already run both traders in USD. In most cases, the cross currency quotes usually incur high costs of transaction.

For example: EUR/GBP, this is called a long-buy, which is the same as to buy a EUR/USD pair and sell it GBP/USD currency pair.

Transaction Cost

A bid/ask spread is an example of a round turn transaction cost. Round turn here we mean a buy or sell trade with the offsetting sell or buy-trades of the equivalent sizes and in the same pair of currencies.

Margin

Every time you come with a new trading account/margin account with brokers, you need to deposit some considerable amount in it. This amount may vary depending on the broker you are investing with. This could go from as small amount as one hundred dollars to one hundred thousand dollars.

Whenever you initiate a trade, there is always a percentage of the balance in your account of that margin account that is put aside and will be used as the initial margin necessity in the upcoming new trade.

Leverage

It is a ratio of capital investment to the needed security deposit. It is also the ability of the trader to take care of huge dollar amounts financial asset using significantly low capital.

It comes in ratios depending on the brokers you are involved with and also the country in which you are trading from. Usually it is in ratios of 500:1 to 2:1 in that order.

All that said and done, we need to embark on how to make money, or money making process in Forex trading. By now, you must be well versed with the technical terminologies as used in the whole of Forex trading and that you are now free to advance your knowledge in other areas comfortably.

Forex trading is much similar to any kind of trade in financial markets for example stocks markets and therefore if you had any prior knowledge of the same, then you stand greater chance sofa learning the trade so easily.

The main agenda of the trade is to trade one currency against the other through exchange with a primary expectation that there will be price changes. What we mean here is that, you will have high hopes that the currency you bought will have its price go higher than the one which you sold for you make some profit.

Example: let's say that you are interested in trading with the US dollar against Euros. Assuming you bought 10,000 US dollars at a rate of 1.1700 and after like one week you realize that the rates of exchange have gone high like say 1.2600 and that you would wish to dispose the money, then you will earn 900 US dollars.

This can be arithmetically represented as follows: EUR 10,000*1.17=US $11,700 and EUR 10,000*1.126=US $12,600.

What Time Do I Need To Buy Or Sell Currencies?

One of the key factors to consider before selecting the currency to trade in is the country of origin of the currency in question. As we know, a currency belongs to a specific country, it originates somewhere there's an economy.

The economy of the country affects the strength or the weight of its currency. So it is good to an economic mapping of the country at which you would with to have their currency traded in before you make any necessary move.

You can do this by conducting what we call Forex fundamental analysis that is usually done by the financial brokers and have the information relayed to the prospective client's f or decision making.

The country's economy may be affected by factors like international trade, lack of employment, general productivity, interest rates as well as manufacturing jus to mention but a few.

Know the Game

We will be showing you an example of how the real trade is done some factors that you need to consider as you initiate the trade.

Suppose you are done with your feasibility study and established that the economy of US is going to weaken, you could decide to initiate a buy EUR/USD. This means that you will have to purchase the Euros with an anticipation that the US dollar will drop in value as compared to the Euro.

You can do the vice versa if you believe that the Euro may weaken in value as compared to the US dollar.

Margin Trading

As we had briefly defined margin before, we now wish to go deeper in the business with margin. You will understand and appreciate the use of margin in Forex trade.

When you need to buy eggs say in a grocery, you will discover that it is hard to get it as one unit, instead they are bundled together, similarly in foreign exchange trade, you will ever find the currencies bundled in the format 1000 or 10,000 to 100,000-units based on your account type and perhaps the type o brokers you are dealing with.

In margin trading, you do not necessarily need to have this entire amount before you trade, you can have capital on borrowed basis called the margin. You are able to go in for greater accounts having very limited capital.

It is very easy to conduct big transactions, efficiently and smoothly even with low initial capital. Assuming the market signals is indicating the rise in pound against the US dollar, you go ahead to open an account placing a lot of say GBP/USD 100,000 units that you have bought by the British pound at a margin of say 2%, you will hence wait as the rates go up.

In this case if bought GBP/US- one lot equivalent to 10,000 units at 1.40000 as the price, it means that you have purchased the 100,000 British Pounds at $140,000 US dollars. Suppose the requirement of the margin was 2 percent, this means that US $2,800 will be spared for opening the trade (2% of $140,000).

This implies that you have the ability to control a lot of 100,000 pounds by use of US $2,800. When the market is favorable to you and you happen to sell of your currencies, you may end up with a closing position of say 1.40500, you will have earned $500. Whatever it is, whether it is a profit or loss is all deposited in your account.

Rollover

Every position that is open at the end of the trading day is rolled over for the next trading period the following day at a fee. We refer this to as rollover fee or interest rate that is either levied to the traders' account or the broker himself. This will be determined by your position and the established margin.

Rollover charges are there on all currencies that are borrowed and therefore used in the trade. However if you wouldn't like to go this extra mile, you only need to ensure that all positions are closed by the close of business each day. Recall that on all borrowed amounts, interest is paid as opposed to earning interest on whatever is bought.

Risk Management

During your first trade with Forex, you do no need to risk a lot of capital to any trade. However, many traders do not bear in mind the kind of risk they are taking as they venture into Forex business instead they put much focus on the size of reward they may get when the business behaves well.

For you to excel in Forex trade, you need to put in to consideration the total amount of money that you need to put at risk in the Forex trading at any single given time. In reality, your effort to manage risks of loses is as essential as your success in maximizing successful trades.

The essence of learning to manage your money that you invest is to gain more profit as you limit risks that could rather lead to loses. There are factors to consider if you want to achieve in this case:

- Recall that Forex trading is fun and enjoyable and because of that you can achieve money easily however, just like any other kind of business, there is a notion of losing. Therefore consider to trade with the money that if lost, you won't be shocked beyond your control.

- You do not need to borrow cash in the process of trading, begin with your savings first, do not go in for leverage and other loans.

- You need to budget well for your investment. Budgeting is one way of enforcing control measures for your business; it helps you stop at a given point if you exhaust the amount that you had placed in for the trade at the close of that day.

Money management requires that you adopt a more conventional trade investment strategy meaning that whatever is available for risking should be part and not the whole business capital.

You are asked to invest sparingly. This is because Forex trade is more of a gambling business where there is no surety of gaining anything instead it is more of a risk than a sure thing. When you are conservative, you will still afford a smile even when things appear to go haywire.

There are very many offers available in this trade. You need to be diversified in your investments. This is a very good strategy in managing your finances. Since there is a lot of volatility in the business as compared to other trades like: stocks trade. However the payouts could vary in relation to the currency pair that you opted in.

You should never place all your eggs in a single basket, is the old saying that has a lot of relevance in this business. In the case of a loss, you need to accept it with joy because it is expected at some point in time. Negative effects may impact your future business decisions drastically.

When you expect a loss, it may act as an eye opener to the investor to point out areas that could act as loopholes and thus enable you to plan well for the future. Loses need to make you become stronger than before and act as leads to your future investments.

You need to begin small and grow with time.-this helps so much especially to beginners. You may be excited and release all your capital to an entire single venture or trade. When you invest sparingly with time, it enables you to gain more stamina in the business as you discipline yourself.

Most Forex brokers accept the smallest minimum sums to begin with. This is a plus to any beginner trader who should be patient as he grows over time. Recall that nothing comes easily. You cannot expect instant marginal gains with your first investment unless it becomes miraculous.

Self-confidence is a plus to any trader. You cannot build confidence in one day that is why you need to invest small sums, watch as they grow, learn how to manage risks and avoid loses then harden up slowly as you increase your trading stock.

There is a direct difference between trading and gambling. Trading is associated with directional or guided or calculated approach in risking that can in the long run offer you best returns and also maintain you in business for quite long.

 Gambling on the other hand is simply a blind risking of your resources with very minimal chances of winning and getting whatever you hope for.

This builds your ability to trade as well taking good care of your mental health. You are not supposed to spent sleepless nights as if you want to win a contract instead you need to stick to a strategy that will yield to proper money management and limiting of loses in your venture.

Trend Analysis and Volatility

The pairs of currency that we trade in foreign exchange trade usually give us the guidelines on the trending lines of the market. This is as a result of high liquidity on daily basis on the market.

There is very many trillions of money that is being traded on daily basis in Forex market which is very high as compared to any other stock markets. Generally all these make up trends for markets. It is very essential to study the trends of the market in order to come up with necessary decisions.

Trendline is a commn tool used that is used for analysis especially in techncal analysis. If well used it can yield a great trading strategy. Sometimes traders draw single trendline that s essential for spoting a historic action of the price other than o rely on probability.

It can also be used to draw lines for market entries and exit. Although most people have ignored the notion of trendlines in repalcement with complex systems or indicators.

Market Expectations

It is quite imperative that for every trader the best language is a profit. however, for forex trading, t quite unpredictable. The trading has got indicators which can aid in definining the trends on the markets.

It is therefore not easy to predict correctly the trends of the market and therefore it is good to have a strong will and shock absorbers in the case of loses.

It is expected that traders in this business remain patient and calm but need to do a lot of research to establish the currencies that are higly liquid to trade in because the business itself is very volatile.

You need to go with signals in order to determine the flow of the market trends available.

Chapter 10: What Is The Best Time To Trade?

Any time of the day is best and suitable to trade in foreign exchange. However there are pros and cons for every time of trade. There are different types of trading times in this event. We have day trading as well as long time trading. We will review the advantage and disadvantage of each of the times in order to set the pace for you.

Both day and long term trading are essential forms of investment of our security and as such, most traders opt for them all. In day trading, trades involved are basically meant to last for a minute or in a twinkle of an eye which takes advantage of instant changes in asset prices.

Positions are opened in the morning and closed at the end of the day, thus, close of business of the very day. This is as opposed to long-term trading where positions are kept open for very long times from weeks to months and even years. They are buying-and –hold oriented trades and not buy-sell ones.

Decision making alone varies from trade to trade especially for the two trades all together. They involve different levels of knowledge and skills or expertise and to some level personality is important.

Swing trading is the middle of the two trades because it spans for a few days through months.

The other difference between day and long term trading or investment is the capital required, time associated with the trade, the level of commitment expected, level of personality and skills and the general returns expected.

These two types are quite important strategies of trade and investment, however the buy and hold investment is more passive in terms of income creation as it is with the day to day trading which is keen on accessing profits on daily basis.

For beginners, there are factors that need to be considered before making up of your mind to what strategy to venture in.

Initial Capital for Investment

For the day-trader of stock especially in the United States, you need a broker account that has got a restricted amount of not less than $25,000 for you to engage in it.

However there is no limit in the minimum balance for you to engage in the day trading for currency markets. You can begin with as little as $1,000. Else if you wish to trade in futures for the day, then the range between: $5,000-$7,500 is highly recommended.

Stock market is good for long term investment. This is so because as for futures, there is an expiry date which makes it not conducive for their trade.

You can also use currencies to trade long term however, but still there is a limitation with options because it is hard to initiate long term trade in this context because of limited and unstable currencies for investment as it is with millions of stocks.

Commissions are another very important aspect to consider before venturing into the trades. Even if the capital requirement to begin the business is not limited, you need to be keen on the commissions which act as additional costs to the investment capital especially if you have less capital.

Different Time Commitment

As with day trading, you will be required to have enough time each day for instance two-hours daily. The first hour speaks a lot especially in the United States for it is the determinant factor for most price changes as opposed to the time after lunch where there activity of the stocks appear to go down.

Day traders have an obligation of reviewing trades every day and every week end. Some day trades will call for active mornings and midnights but if you find that these are not convenient times for you, and then you can opt for the long-term trades.

Relevant Skills and Personality

You need to commit your time to trading through research and strategizing on what will work for you well. This is for every type of trade in securities. There is also a need to spend much time learning on how to put in practice the strategies learned because, for new traders, they tend to shift their attention and emotionally to concentrating on the invested capital.

All these types' f investments need patience but in different measures altogether. As for day traders, they are so active and deal in several trades per day even if they have to monitor triggers for the buy and sell to happen before they actually trade.

Benefits of Journal and or Diary Keeping

A journal or a diary may be differentiated by the names. However the primary objective is to have record of events and business happenings at different intervals.

There are several reasons why journals are very essential especially in Forex trading. We will be reviewing a few of them in the next paragraph.

1. To Have Organized Thoughts

Diaries are records for the organization of our thoughts and apprehension. Records can be kept for the daily occurrences, events, feeling and thoughts concerning different happenings of the day. A journal will enable you to mark and store the entries sin your diary.

2. Enhance your Writing

You need to train writing by making journals. It helps you improve the quality of writing. It doesn't matter where you have a smart topic or not. It is as easy as putting your thought in journeys. You will improve your writing as you advance in journaling.

3. For Emergency Situations

Perhaps you ever needed to remind yourself of what you could have done on a specific day in time, and then the journal could be the best answer to this question. For example: lawsuits, this is characterized by some event and perhaps any necessary decision that could be invaluable for you today. In case of any emergency, you may wish to get some guideline to that.

4. Tracking Vital Decisions Made

As a trader, you need to remind yourself of the decisions that you make in different situations that can be helpful for your future decision making process. This can be available only on journals if kept. As we know, business is an ongoing concern and as such, decisions made today may be helpful in the future suppose a similar event occurs.

5. Interaction with other People

As a business person, interactions with other people could be very beneficial and because of that, you need to keep track and relevant record of the interactions which may become beneficial in future to you and your business.

You may tend to review the kind of support and opinions that you were given by people in the past and seems relevant in the current trading period.

6. Monitor your Progress

It is very important to take into consideration your progress in business, this call for a record of events as they occurred from the beginning to the present.

As you know, growth is not an overnight business and therefore along the way, you could have encountered some mishaps that maybe acted as stepping stones to your current status. You would need to review them in order to correct your current or rejoice in your current situation depending on the current status.

7. Recall What You Were From Before

We can refer this to as personal story. Every event, decision and people that affected your life must be remembered. They form your story and therefore it is good if they appeared in your journal. A journal is very accurate in its context and very complete which makes it completely useful.

If you can recall what and who you were and perhaps your previous standing could help you to avoid some mistakes that were done in the past.

8. Give Credit to Your Life

Everyone needs to make his life meaningful. This concept is so subjective in nature. You may have had some dreams, anticipations, hopes or projections of which without a proper track, they could be long lost along the way. If you have a proper journal, you could follow them up to ensure you accomplish them.

9. Daily Thoughts And Self-Realization

You need to have introspection through a journal as a way of preserving your skills and becoming so compassionate person.

10. Stress Relief

It is so important to note down your feelings or anxieties, this in other words it is called brain-draining. It makes you end the day on a good note and feel so very light in your mind. It also gives you room to meditate and think of new ideas and new agendas.

This releases your pressure and stress from your head that you could have kept. You are left to be happy and rejuvenate.

11. Improve your Brain Memory Capacity

In general, your brain tends to keep record of every occurrence in our lives. However, to aid recall well, you need to boost it with a written down point of reference. Suppose you learned an idea and put it down on paper, it becomes easier for the brain to connect and reflect on it. It makes the process of remembrance easier and quite effective.

Chapter 11: Understanding the Role of Brokers

Brokers are established companies that offer trading platforms to trader which help them to buy or sell foreign monies. Most transitions in this particular market are conducted between pars of currencies and therefore traders buy or either sells a certain pair of their own choice.

In other words, Forex brokers are actors acting as intermediaries or the central man between the seller and the buyer of the foreign currencies. They act as intermediaries and therefore earn some commission whenever the trade has been initiated.

He is very independent and is used widely by various institutions or individuals to do business in the foreign exchange market.

His primary role is join the sellers with the buyers for trade to go on, in the same case, he provides both parties with markets information, say products, current trend, prices, and any other related market conditions.

Some Forex brokers are known by Forex retailing brokers and also they could be called currency-trading

Forex brokers. Only a small volume of the entire Forex market is held or run by a single Forex firm. Forex retailers have a 24-hour access to the entire Forex market for speculation purposes.

Brokerage services as well are given to institutional clients through large and well established firms such as commercial banks. There are some key concepts that you need to know as you continue in this venture as a Forex investor or scholar.

- Forex brokers enable their Forex traders to have access to Forex markets in order to trade in currencies.

- Brokers, mostly serve retailer clients as opposed to institutional clients who are ever served by large and well established firms.

- Brokers assist their clients with leverage services for them to trade with.

- Most brokers locally make their monies in many ways including the bid-ask spreads.

What Is The Role Of a Forex Broker?

A real foreign exchange broker enables a trader to have access to all currency-pairs which are ever on market like the USD/JPY, EUR/USD and many other currency pairs just to mention but a few with every rates for exchange available on market.

They go ahead to enable their clients to trade in them most current currency markets. He will ensure to initiate the trade by enabling the customer to acquire by buying of the currency pairs and help him to sell them at the same time.

Assuming clients have an interest in trading the US dollars against the Euros, then the broker will lead the client to trade in that pair thus EUR/USD. This means that, Euros will be purchased by use of US dollars significantly.

Similarly, to close the business, the client will be supposed to trade off the Euros for the US dollars in that order. For the trader to make a profit, it means that he has to dispose of the purchased amount when the exchange rates are higher than when he bought them or else he will settle for a loss.

Brokers however have drastically improved their services to its clients over time. Because of this, you can simply open an account for foreign trading in very simple steps online. You will be required by your broker to make some deposits on your account as collateral before you proceed to the real trade.

The amount you trade in is not limited to what you deposited on your account because the brokers will offer you with leverage in order to trade in large sums of money than the initial deposit.

This is entirely dependent on the trader's country of operation, which means that the leverage can go up between thirty and four hundred times as much of the initial capital as leverage. The more the leverage, the higher the risk and this are what most traders find themselves in.

Advantages of Using Brokers

They have a vast network of markets and well connections to the industries that investors do not know by their own ability. As intermediaries, they are equipped with tools and resources for accessing larger markets of sellers and buyers of products.

They have established rapports with commercial banks and related financial tools which in the long run empower them finically. They are not as costly as it could be with the case if the client went in to find the resources and the market for their products.

Brokers in the recent past could only work with tycoons because of their costs for operations. The emergency of the internet has made it so easy for the online-brokers to offer substantial rates to the clients even if they don't give access to any customized information to clients.

How Do Forex Brokers Earn?

There are two basic ways in which they make up their money. First and foremost, we have what is referred to as the bid-ask spread. A real bid-ask spread looks like this: assuming the traders is trading with the US dollars versus the Euros, and the prices are 1.20020 for the bid and 1.20034 for the-ask, then it means that the spread in this particular pair is 0.00014.

Now, suppose the client opened a position at the ask price of which at the end closed the same position at the bid price, it means that the spread amount will be collected by the broker as his earning.

The second way is through imposing of extra fees or money to cater for their pay. They may charge the amount either on every transaction handled or even on a monthly basis for the access to their trading user interface.

On the other hand, you will find that nowadays, Forex brokers are very many and as such, there is too much competition. Because of completion, brokers are forced to cut down most of their fees that they impose on clients in order to capture a market for the clientele. They are therefore limited to the spread amounts only and meager transaction costs.

Some of them go ahead to gain money from their own operations. If there is a conflict or interest with clients, it means that they lose on the transaction fees but this problem has been limited greatly in the recent past.

How to Invest With Brokers

Forex trade on the exchange market is a hobby that needs passion and a stable income or financial resources. There are many billions to trillions that cross hands every single day on the securities market and the Forex market respectively. For example: approximately $22.5 billion for securities and $5.1 trillion for foreign currencies in that order.

In order to begin with Forex trading, you first of all need to find a broker. Brokers are all over and as fresher you may find it a task finding the best that suits your needs well. Some of them will give you an opportunity to test their platforms through demo accounts.

You Need To Open an Account with a Broker

This is the first step in beginning the Forex trading exercise. In order to get an account with the brokers which are more like any normal bank account, it requires some bits of paper work. The whole process may take some days to be complete.

For those of you who may be interested with demonstrations, the brokers offer such facilities as demo accounts which you can use for training and testing the waters. You only need very limited information and the account will be open.

This will in turn provide you with relevant practical skills and knowledge to empower you before launching deep into real business.

They Provide Leverage

This service is available to every account holder and the amount varies according to the country and perhaps the type of account you hold and the broker firms you are dealing with. It comes in ratios of "10:1 across 100:1".

This means that whatever amount that you have on your account can be increased ten times or a hundred times before trading. The actual amount on your account is actually stepped up in the ratio given before accessing the market.

For instance, if you had $400 US dollars on your account, in the first ratio of 10:1, the amount that will be exposed to trading will be $400*10 that is $4000 US dollars. Now, leverage has its advantages as well as the disadvantages.

You can gain great profits and at the same time you can end up in very big loses. Every Forex brokers must educate its clients on this knowledge as it is as requirement by the law. For those traders who get so much excited about the deal, they jump in very quickly but at the end of the day, they weep aloud.

You Need To Balance Your Equation

As long as you are working with foreign exchange brokers, you need to consider two distinct balances available to your account. The first one is your original account balance excluding the open trades. The other balance is what you get after all your traders have been closed and the net balance as your second balance.

Bid Ask Spread

If you open a trade with Forex brokers, the trade will be taken to the market on your behalf. In the due course, they will supply you with the prices for the currency pairs which is a bit varied from the price they will find o market.

They normally display it in ratios like EUR/USD1.20025/1.20035 which literally signifies that the first figure is the amount that the broker offers you when you wish to sell-off your pair.

The second figure stands for the amount of commission that is charged by the broker suppose you want to buy the currency pair. For this case, $USD 0.00010 is the difference and that is the commission for the broker. Based on the trading demand and supply, the spread may narrow down or even widen.

The difference in the bid-ask spread is the charge ever referred to as the collecting spread. Such charges are quite open to every trader. In addition, you need to be aware that the leveraged amount is where the spread is captured and not on your account.

Education on the Forex Trade

Forex trading is quite new in reality to many new investors. Information on the price of the stocks could have significant effect on the general prices of the currencies to trade in. pricing of currencies and investment is a lesson that is never attractive to new investors.

Lack of sufficient knowledge is a drawback to investors and therefore most brokers have made it easy for their potential clients to acquire knowledge to be empowered before they usher them in to the real business. Nothing is done on assumptions due to the uniqueness of the Forex trading itself.

Broker's Reputation Should Be Verified

Through Forex brokers, you are able to get links to various banking institutions which offer opportunities for trading with several currencies. There are a set of guidelines that are being followed to run their operations.

In the recent past, many Forex brokers were never regulated but as for now, there are restrictions, rules and laws that govern their daily operations, however you may find that some brokerages have better reputations as compared to others.

There is an association which provides the reputations of all existing Forex-broker firms that can be conducted before choosing the firm of your interest. It is called: "National-Futures-Association".

Meta Trader 4 Platform

This is the ever referred as the best Forex trading platform. It offers the most sophisticated and most current analytical tools and technology in addition to other services. As they say, it has got all that you need for Forex trade. It helps you to execute strategies of all sorts of complexity.

This platform as offered by the broker firms has got very many free already paid for signals that have got various risk as well as profitability levels running on both demo and actual accounts simultaneously and at your disposal.

This is to say that, it has got very many providers all a long; it has got hundreds of thousand s of strategies for trading as well as trading conditions. Their nature of built-in markets offers it as the bets platform for many Expert-Advisors or the latest indicators.

One of its most interesting features is the ability to send financial alert news and information to clients who use such to plan for the inevitable in the price changes and as such make right decisions for trading.

www.ingramcontent.com/pod-product-compliance
Lightning Source LLC
Chambersburg PA
CBHW070345220526
45467CB00001B/248